# THE HOUSEKEEPER
## [La Donna di Governo]

CARLO GOLDONI

# MIRANDOLINA
## [La Locandiera]

# THE HOUSEKEEPER
## [La Donna di Governo]

### TRANSLATED BY
### ROBERT DAVID MACDONALD

These translations first published by Oberon Books Limited, 521 Caledonian Road, London N7 9RH.
Tel: 071 607 3637/Fax: 071 607 3629

Printed by Multiplex Medway Ltd

ISBN 1 870259 48 3

Cover design: Andrzej Klimowski

For Andy Wilde

*A champion Goldonian from a Goldoni champion*

# INTRODUCTION

The craft of the playwright depends on fashion as much as that of the couturier: in each case some follow and some lead, but both depend on immediate public approval. Theatrical reputations are therefore more subject to market fluctuation even than political reputations; the previous generation's judgment may go out-of-date but still hangs around, like those suspect bottles of tablets that accumulate at the back of the bathroom cabinet long after their use-by date. One such opinion which could well have been flushed away by now is the evaluation of Goldoni, by nearly all countries other than his own, as the author of anything between two and five hundred comedies, all with happy endings and all exactly the same.

In the year of the bicentenary of his death (1993), which passed more or less unnoticed by the British theatre, this book presents two of his plays, one of them certainly his best-known, the other arguably his least-known, in an attempt to right the balance in favour of a playwright who was among the most versatile of his century, in whose work we find odd, fleeting traces of future authors, and who, so far from being the high priest of the happy ending, was, like Marivaux, whom he resembles much more closely than he does Molière, to whom he is constantly and invidiously compared, more a master of the ironic ending. The sexual duel is uneasily resolved, conditions for a quiet life are laid down which permanently preclude contentment, war takes its usual coarsening toll of people's hearts and minds, and the wages of sin may well turn out to be a good annual income and a respectable address. One of these plays has what it is possible to recognise as a happy ending in the eighteenth-century manner; in the other, the implications of the conclusion, based on the venality of those concerned, are cynical, heartless and amoral.

Goldoni's life (1707-1793) has a symmetry worthy of one of his better plots. Born seven years after the start of the century, he died seven years before the end of it: he spans the century, a small area of whose surface he faultlessly reflected, and during which he effected a double reform, freeing the Italian theatre from the pompous erudition of the academic theatre, and the gratuitous buffoonery of the popular. During the twenty years on each side of the half-century he produced his most enduring and endearing work, speaking first and foremost for Venice, a city famous for her understanding of Man's need to amuse himself. The attractive capital of an unattractive empire whose last colony had vanished a generation before (1716), Venice still boasted sixteen theatres at a time when Paris had four and London two. Like Casanova, his contemporary and compatriot, Goldoni survived into the age of Robespierre and de Sade, puzzled, exiled and disillusioned, each of them writing, in a step-mother tongue, autobiographies unrivalled in their century for wit, charm, sparkle and sheer inaccuracy.

Unlike Casanova, whose life was his material, Goldoni's material was his life, about which, apart from that material, there is little to relate of much interest; working authors do not have much time to lead interesting lives, and Goldoni is at pains in his memoirs to preserve a polite decorum and, as befits a playwright, to place himself in the best position and in the best, most amiable light. All this, allied to a conveniently selective memory, make the memoirs a primary source as misleading as they are entertaining. It goes some way in mitigation to remember that people tend to lie largely because other people expect too much of them.

Born in Venice, February 25th, 1707, to Giulio Goldoni and his some-what older and more than somewhat richer wife, Margherita (Salvioni), Carlo studied law somewhat erratically, achieving his degree at Padua in 1731, fell in and, "with equal facility", out of love several times, behaving otherwise with only a faint raffishness to ruffle the well-conducted surface of code-bound Venetian bourgeois society. Meanwhile he was inching towards the theatre: at eleven, the year after his father completed his medical studies, he performed at school in the female lead of Gigli's *La Sorellina* and, we are assured, wrote a comedy. At fourteen, a memorable boat-trip with a theatre troupe from Rimini to Chioggia left him in little doubt of the company he preferred. Later came a satire, for which he was expelled from school, an opera, *Amalasunta*, which he burnt after it was rejected by the Milan Opera, an interlude *Il Gondoliere Veneziano*, written for a celebrated scholar, physician, intellectual, stage manager and moun-tebank, Bonafede Vitali, and finally, commissioned by one of Vitali's actors, a tragedy, *Belisario*. An undistinguished piece, it is nevertheless important as marking Goldoni's decisive commitment to a profession which allowed him to do what he wanted to do, with people he liked, and be paid for it.

He started as resident dramatist, more probably what we would recognise as dramaturg, of the Giuseppe Imer company, in which, incidentally, Casanova's mother, La Buranella, was a leading actor. After a slowish start, some twelve years and fifteen plays later, and by then a married man, he moved to the Sant' Angelo theatre with Girolamo Medebac and his wife Teodora, with a contract to write eight comedies and two operas a year, not to write for any other company (except for musical plays) and to accompany the troupe on tour between Carnival and the beginning of the autumn season in Venice. Goldoni stayed with them for five years, writing some forty-five plays for them. In 1750 - the half-way mark of his symmetrical life - following the not entirely satisfactory conclusion of a literary squabble with another playwright, the Abbé Chiari, and the threatened departure of the company's leading actor after a declining season, Goldoni undertook, in a sonnet recited by the leading actress on the last night of Carnival, to write sixteen plays for the next theatrical year, one for every week of the season. Bets, and in some quarters hopes, ran high that he would fail, and, indeed, when autumn came only seven out of the sixteen comedies had been written. More than once during the year Goldoni had to start rehearsing the first act before the other acts were finished, but he kept his promise, with, astoundingly, only two flops, and an amazingly high proportion of first-class work.

It did his health no good, though, and widened an already existing rift between him and the Medebac management, which resulted in his moving, in 1753, to the Teatro San Luca, managed by the aloof and patrician Vendramin brothers, with whom he stayed for his last ten years in Venice; the decade was one of almost continual worry of one kind and another, but in it Goldoni managed to produce, among some seventy-odd plays, his most accomplished work.

Back in Venice in 1758 after a short and unsuccessful stint in Rome, where women were still not allowed on the stage, he became involved in one of those resoundingly pointless theatrical pamphlet wars to which middle-aged dramatists seem peculiarly prone - how do Writers' Unions ever start? - this time with Giuseppe Baretti, a freebooting literary thug of no real account, but with a one-man periodical, and, more importantly, with Count Carlo Gozzi.

It is hard to imagine, in an age of media diversification, the intensity of such cultural squabbles, though anyone who remembers the polemics for and against the "Angry Young Men" of the mid-1950s may recall a faint whiff of what they must have been like. Otherwise they are as hard to understand as the various operatic feuds - Gluck versus Piccini, Haendel versus Bononcini, Wagner-Liszt versus Brahms-Hanslick; with every generation the combatants become less and less easy to tell apart. (Even while the Haendel-Bononcini duel was actually being fought, a London lampoon ran "Strange that such difference should be ("Twixt Tweedledum and Tweedledee!") Nowadays, theatrical uproar, in Britain at any rate, is prompted almost solely by sexual scandal, mostly initiated and inevitably over-orchestrated by ancillary media: the result of the gradual process of making the theatre primarily a middle-class entertainment, which began with the knighting of Henry Irving and continues relatively unchecked. In Goldoni's Venice, the cessation of empire had brought on a petrifaction of society and government; the ruling oligarchy was shrinking, and not allowing itself to be absorbed into the bourgeoisie, as, for example, in Austrian Lombardy, but closing in on itself and guarding ever more jealously its political privileges. Any rebellion against the government was likely to be a rebellion against the modernisation of governmental formulae and an appeal for the re-establishment of the traditional constitution - revolution was regressive.

This feeling was bound to have an effect on cultural life. The Italians, with other Mediterranean nations, have always had an ample share of morbidity, and a more than ample share of foreign invasion, by armies either of soldiers or tourists, to both of which they have reacted with an amiable contempt, and settled back to convert the missionaries. There is not a nation in the West today that does not bear, in its painting, its poetry, its music, its clothes, its cooking and its car design, the indelible stamp of the last millenium of an Italian culture that has maintained itself largely independent of outside influence, an example of one-way pollination impossible in nature and unique in Western civilisation. Only the Chinese, on the other side of the planet, have managed the same *tour de force* of dissemination without diminution. There is, however, a price-tag on such isolationism; here the decline of Venice furnished an occasion where the Italians really could with advantage have taken a leaf from a neighbour's book, namely the European, especially the French Enlightenment, and they failed to do so. One advantage of living in a period of decadence is, or should be, that one can express oneself on any subject more or less as one likes; empires have not grown strong on listening to the other man's point of view. The danger is when the system begins to ossify rather than liquefy, thus putting paid to any chance of smooth transition.

Goldoni, at the start of his career, had found the traditional Italian comedy of masks, a ritual sunk, like all rituals that have outlived their immediate attraction, usefulness or cultural viability, into a vehicle for virtuosity and charm at best, and at worst into an excuse for pandering to the lowest common factor in its audience: he had taken it and wrested from it the eighteenth-century Comedy of Manners, insisting that actors spoke his lines, not theirs, relegating the use of masks to subsidiary characters, and finally getting rid of them altogether. The radicalism of this move, in the eyes of actors and public alike, can hardly be understood today, but it lies at the heart of the Goldoni-Gozzi dispute, which was not merely about form, but about the introduction of a radical shift in morals as well.

The Venetian government was pedantic in its supervision of all activities, public and private, of its subjects; it intervened continually in the literary polemics of these years, banning performances of Goldoni's *Crafty Widow* and Chiari's *School for Widows* in 1749, censoring a scene of Goldoni's in which a nobleman seduces, or tries to seduce a woman with a promise of marriage, and encouraged Gozzi in his attack on Goldoni, provided it did not come "to blows". In such a climate, Gozzi, the aristocratic amateur, contrasted strikingly with the bourgeois professional Goldoni, the one intransigent in his determination to preserve the theatre from modernism and reform, the other open to every innovative idea; they could hardly have been more different, both as men and as writers. Gozzi himself insisted that his own work, a revival of the masked, semi-improvised comedy in a series of attractively presented fairy tales, was a counter-reformation of Goldoni's reform, moved by the conviction that Goldoni's work contained implicit political and social positions that imperilled the structure of Church and State. If Goldoni, though rooted in his own century, represented in a certain sense the future, Gozzi was a dinosaur, a survivor from the past, an archetype in a Venice which would, in a few years, crumble without being able to reform itself.

In 1762, quite suddenly, if we are to believe the Memoirs, but in fact as the product of gradual and mounting disillusion with Venice, as much with Vendramin, his employer, as with Gozzi, (though he was caused more grief by these polemics than he ever confessed - the Memoirs are strangely reticent on the subject) Goldoni bade the city - and his audience - a moving farewell in *One of the Last Evenings of Carnival* and set off for Paris, a better salary with the management of the second-rate Theatre Italien, and artistic bankruptcy. Many artists are so tied to their native lands that they wither outside them - one thinks of Prokofieff preferring to work under the strictures of Zhdanov inside Russia than fritter away his genius untrammelled in the United States - and none more so than Goldoni, faultless reporter and chronicler of a few square miles in the armpit of the Adriatic. His ignorance of French customs was extensive, his ignorance of the French language almost complete, his ignorance of the French spirit profound. But Paris meant change, and it meant escape, even if it also meant a step backwards, precipitating him once more into the sort of theatre he had spent his whole working life reforming. For the next thirty years, his decline is rapid and depressing to witness. He was never at home in Paris, his plays were only sporadically successful, and even more infrequently of any real quality, his eventual sinecure as teacher of Italian to the Dauphine Adelaide tedious and barely more rewarding financially than spiritually, and his health and eyesight were going fast. If the morning had been golden, the evening was lead.

If there is one thing the human race can call its own it is the joke, an irrational by-passing of rational communication, which is denied to animals and probably to angels as well. It also appears to be denied to revolutionaries, whose time is usually too precious to be taken up by such anodynes, signs of a leisure few of them can afford, and which most of them are dedicated to destroy. The French Revolutionary government, running true to form, refused to restore Goldoni's pension, admittedly a royal gift, preferring to subsidise more improving authors. Now blind, but nursed by a wife as devoted as she had been patient, his last years were spent in poverty and ill-health. Finally Marie-Joseph Chénier, brother of André, and himself a playwright, eloquently persuaded the Convention to reverse its decision, but Goldoni had died two days before. The Convention tried to make some amends by ordering a benefit performance for Nicoletta, his widow, but it was too late. While mankind prefers to bestow its applause on its destroyers rather than its benefactors, it is just as well someone should be there to laugh at them; but they can hardly expect much reward for doing so. Or not on earth.

Neither of the plays in this book was written in Venetian dialect, a fact that need not disturb the English reader. Goldoni's Tuscan Italian was not elegant; as he admits, "although my plays had been first published in Florence under the eyes and the censorship of the learned men of the country... I was always reproached with the original sin of Venetianism." It is only in his dialect comedies that he achieves real distinction of style. Nevertheless his language appears deceptively easy, as effortless as his technique of never saying more than is necessary for an actor to build on: a conventional response, filtered through the actor's personality can evoke a world of meaning, and Goldoni's asides are often no more than indications (not necessarily spoken) of behaviour and reaction. An accomplished opera librettist - he wrote for Haydn, Mozart, and Vivaldi among others - he knew the dangers of the unsupervised prima donna, but he also understood instinctively that an actor of quality can say more with a platitude and a shrug, than many more respected authors can with an attitude and a dozen heroic couplets.

These two plays are studies, from alarmingly divergent angles, of women, (a field where Goldoni excelled), both of them servants, an inn-keeper and a housekeeper, surviving precariously in a man's world. One operates in a public situation where open dealing is a prerequisite of her profession - as the Chinese adage says "He who has not smiling face, should not open shop"- the other in an entirely private situation, where intrigue is essential to having one's cake and eating it. One is the target of numerous suitors who range from the ludicrous to the loyal, by way of materialism and misogyny; the other, herself both materialistic and misanthropic, picks her own sexual targets to achieve her self-seeking but also self-preserving ends. Along the way, both of them come near to calamity in their dealings with the sex whose approval is necessary to their continued survival as equals in a world where they have no equality - merely certain advantages.

Of all Goldoni's plays, *Mirandolina* (La Locandiera, 1753) needs least introduction to English readers. The title role, the impeccable clockwork of the scenario, the quasi-satisfactory conclusion of the sexual square-dance, (if such conclusions can *ever* be satisfactory) have carried the play to more performances all over the world, than the rest of Goldoni's work put together. Goldoni himself had no particular affection for the play, the labour of no more than two months, and barely any for the heroine, whom he thought he was putting in the dock to stand in for a number of actresses he had known in and out of the theatre. Discretion, indeed, made it necessary, or at least desirable, for him to set the action in Florence rather then Venice, where it clearly belongs.

Mirandolina is an extension of Colombina, the commedia dell'arte stereotype of the artful servant, the working-class girl putting her social superiors, unused to her street tactics, firmly in their place: it is instructive to compare her to her male equivalents, such as Sancho Panza or Leporello, who are continually placed in humiliating positions by their employers. Inheriting the hotel on her father's death, she is ambitious to run it herself without the need for marriage: like Elizabeth I, she knows virginity to be a formidable diplomatic advantage. She is economical (she does not give unknown guests the best sheets), practical (she is her own accountant and an excellent cook) and tactful (she keeps her more demonstratively amorous guests at arms' length). Into this carefully balanced, if rather conventional circle there intrudes an attractive young man who is not remotely attracted to her as a woman, a situation unknown to her as yet.

It is always a shock the first time one is turned down, and maybe the younger we are when it happens, the better. In the same way that collectors of almost anything yield to the schoolboy urge to complete a series, Mirandolina, yielding also to the common female illusion that misogynists are simply men who haven't yet found the right woman, determines to save the young man from his convictions. She succeeds, but in such a way that she herself is exposed to the risk of being drawn into an attachment she is unwilling to carry through: to break the spell, she reveals the trick, and the young man retreats, snarling, into the broken fragments of his shell, an unusual fate, it must be admitted, for the hero of an eighteenth-century comedy, even when he can be identified with its author. It is noticeable how, after his dismissal, the fizz seems to go out of the bottle for Mirandolina: she realises how narrow, almost Pyrrhic, her victory has been, how dangerous and unattractive the games she has been playing, and she uses her lucky, if not complete, escape, to hurry along the conclusion which is, we realise only at the moment it happens, the fitting one, the one we were waiting for all along - stagecraft of no mean order.

(Incidentally, the parts of the two actresses, generally cut nowadays as dead wood dramatically, and certainly financially, are one more example of Goldoni's economy of staging; their rapacious technique with men shows Mirandolina a better way to go about things, enabling her to achieve what could be seen as a somewhat unsympathetic end by sympathetic means. If, at the same time, Goldoni could snipe at the odd outmoded theatrical convention, so much the better)

The Housekeeper (La Donna di Governo), written five years later (1758), is quite another kettle of fish, and it is easy to see why it has not attained the popularity of the earlier play. The open-air feeling there, where people's behaviour is, to some extent, conditioned by what may be done in public, is exchanged for the closed-in atmosphere of a family apartment, tyrannised over by its oldest member, himself a slave to his obsession for a woman. We are meeting with Colombina again, but what a difference! Where Mirandolina kept her lovers at arms' length, Valentina is at pains to keep hers within arms' reach. Where Mirandolina is putting off marriage to avoid, among other things, a division of property she already owns, Valentina is grasping at marriage as "the bribe" as Thornton Wilder puts it, "to make a housekeeper think she's a householder". Where Mirandolina ends up making the sensible choice - commercially as well, getting herself a husband and a business partner at the same time, Valentina ends up with both the lovers she was determined to have, feeling for one what the other feels for her, and supporting one on the proceeds of the other. It would take a hardened cynic to see a happy ending there. When we get what we want, we get it in the form we deserve. None of the characters is in any way admirable, or even attractive, except, perhaps, the two young lovers, who are too stupid to be wicked (or attractive for that matter), and the baleful presence of Valentina throws the detailed family relationships, which Goldoni was always expert at portraying, into sharp relief.

It is always a temptation, and nearly always a mistake, to compare one artist to another, and the comparison of Goldoni with Molière, as obstinate as it is ill-judged, does neither any good; similarly, to present him as a harbinger of the drama of the future equally diminishes him. All the same, it may not be too far-fetched to see the shadow of The Housekeeper falling across Ibsen's desk. Goldoni, in this play, was manipulating the stereotypes until a comedy could be made from the material of domestic tragedy. And that was something Ibsen never managed. The ending, with its clear implications of a ménage à trois is as daring as anything in Strindberg. Goldoni was adamant about drawing a veil over impropriety of manners and decorum, but, like Marivaux, he took care the veil should be fairly transparent.

The memoirs are clear on what its author, twenty years later, thought of the play: "I shall not enlarge on the piece, which, from its mediocrity, is altogether undeserving of any such notice... whether from the defect of the subject or the execution, the piece failed at its first presentation and was instantly withdrawn." This seems both bilious and unfair, even if the rhyming verse of the play is often awkward, Goldoni never being at his best either in verse or in Tuscan Italian, but clearly failure rankled at a time when he was used to success, and he never rewrote it in prose, as he had done with a number of other, more successful comedies - *The Impresario from Smyrna*, *The Good-Humoured Ladies* and others - which is my justification for having produced a prose version here.

*"There is a great deal of good in Lord Augustus.*
*Fortunately it is all on the surface. Just where*
*good qualities should be."*
(Oscar Wilde: Lady Windermere's Fan Act II)

The world and work of Goldoni are as interlinked as they must be if an artist's work is to survive his world. All great writers give the illusion of having created a superficial world complete in every detail - Dickens, Proust, Mann - when they have, in fact, selected only those surfaces we need to be aware of: the whole, as with, say, Zola or Galsworthy, being quite indigestible.

Goldoni is the master of the superficial; which is all the theatre can show. We can see actors and hear them; we cannot know, however educated our guess, what they are thinking. As with the characters in the novels of Raymond Chandler, it is always "I said..." or "I did..." never "I thought..." It is this immediacy, this spontaneity that give Goldoni his particular flavour, and which can make him, it must be admitted, sometimes seem pretty thin on the page, where the leisure we are denied in the theatre makes us ask for a profundity which is not Goldoni's intention. What you see is what you get. Surface is all; the miracle is that it can show so much and imply still more.

There are more than a hundred and fifty plays. A bare thirty of them have been performed anywhere this century. Perhaps by the time the tercentenary of Goldoni's birth (2007) comes round, a few more will have entered the repertoire.

RDM Glasgow 1993

# MIRANDOLINA
## [La Locandiera]

# CHARACTERS

The MARCHESE of Forlipopoli
The CONTE of Albafiorita
FABRIZIO, a servant in the inn
The CAVALIERE of Ripafratta
MIRANDOLINA, innkeeper
STEFANO, servant to the Cavaliere
ORTENSIA, an actress
DEJANIRA, another actress

The action passes in Mirandolina's inn in Florence

This translation of *Mirandolina* was first produced at the Citizens' Theatre, Glasgow in 1976, directed by Robert David MacDonald and designed by Philip Prowse, with the following cast:

The Marchese, *Jonathan Hyde*
The Conte, *Laurance Rudic*
Fabrizio, *Philip Bloomfield*
The Cavaliere, *David Hayman*
Stefano, *Stephen Petcher*
Mirandolina, *Suzanne Bertish*
Ortensia, *Julia Blalock*
Dejanira, *Jill Spurrier*

This revised version was first presented at the Lyric Theatre, Hammersmith in 1994, directed by Delia Ibelhauptaite and designed by Ashley Martin-Davis, with the following cast:

The Marchese, *Tim McMullen*
The Conte, *Graham Turner*
Fabrizio, *Robert Goodale*
The Cavaliere, *Reece Dinsdale*
Stefano, *Thomas Browne*
Mirandolina, *Caroline Quentin*

# ACT ONE

## SCENE 1

MARCHESE: Between you and me there yawns a considerable social gulf.

CONTE: My money's as good as yours at this inn.

MARCHESE: But if the landlady pays me rather more attention, that is only suitable in my case rather than yours.

CONTE: And why should you think that, pray?

MARCHESE: I am the Marchese of Forlipopoli.

CONTE: And I am the Conte of Albafiorita.

MARCHESE: Exactly. Anyone can buy a title, Conte.

CONTE: And anyone can sell an estate, Marchese.

MARCHESE: Enough! I am a person of standing. And accustomed to be used with respect.

CONTE: Oh, indeed, while you can behave to everybody with a familiarity which...

MARCHESE: I am staying at this inn because I am in love with the proprietress. Everyone is aware of this and everyone should respect a young woman of whom I approve.

CONTE: What on earth do you think I am doing here in Florence? Why do you imagine I am putting up at, and with, this disgusting inn?

MARCHESE: You will get nowhere.

CONTE: And you will?

MARCHESE: Indeed and indeed. I am a person of standing. Mirandolina needs my protection.

CONTE: Mirandolina needs money.

MARCHESE: I have no lack of that.

CONTE: I spend a guinea a day in this place. Not to speak of the presents I give her all the time.

MARCHESE: I don't need to brag of what I spend.

CONTE: No, indeed not, since everyone knows.

MARCHESE: Oh, no they don't.

CONTE: Oh, yes, they do. *Caro* Signor Marchese, servants talk. Two shillings a day, am I right - at most?

MARCHESE: Servants! Fabrizio! Can't abide the man. And I fancy our hostess has a soft spot for the wretched creature.

CONTE: Perhaps she wants to marry him. No bad thing, either. Her father's dead and this place is too much for a woman on her own. In point of fact, I've promised her three hundred pounds if she gets married.

MARCHESE: If she marries, I am the one who will be protecting her and giving... well, I shall know how to behave.

CONTE: Listen... Let us agree as between friends. Let us each give her three hundred - equal shares, you follow me?

MARCHESE: What I do I shall perform by stealth, with no need to boast. I am a person of standing. [*Calling*] Is anybody there!

CONTE: (Ruined! No pride like a poor man's!)

FABRIZIO: [*Entering, to the MARCHESE*] Signore?

MARCHESE: Signore? Who taught you manners, boy?

FABRIZIO: Beg your pardon.

CONTE: Fabrizio! How is your mistress?

FABRIZIO: Very well, *Illustrissimo*.

MARCHESE: Is she up yet?

FABRIZIO: Yes, *Illustrissimo*.

MARCHESE: Impudent rascal!

FABRIZIO: *Illustrissimo*?

MARCHESE: What do you mean, *Illustrissimo*?

FABRIZIO: It's what I called the other gentleman.

MARCHESE: Between him and me there is a considerable difference.

CONTE: [*To FABRIZIO*] You hear that?

FABRIZIO: (In the matter of tips, anyway)

MARCHESE: Tell your mistress to come and see me. I wish to speak to her.

FABRIZIO: Yes, *Eccellenza*. Am I right this time?

MARCHESE: You've known perfectly well for three months now: but you're an impertinent wretch.

FABRIZIO: Always happy to oblige, *Eccellenza*.

CONTE: Would you like to see the real difference between the Marchese and me?

MARCHESE: What's that supposed to mean?

CONTE: Here. A guinea for you. Get another from him.

FABRIZIO: Thank you, *Illustrissimo*. [*To MARCHESE*] *Eccellenza*...

MARCHESE: I don't throw my money away like a lunatic. Get out!

FABRIZIO: Heaven bless you, *Illustrissimo*. [*To MARCHESE*] *Eccellenza* (If you want proper service abroad, it's money counts over titles).

[*He goes out*]

MARCHESE: You think you're going to come over me with gifts, but you won't get anywhere. My rank outweighs all your money.

CONTE: I'm not arguing about what it's worth, but what will it buy?

MARCHESE: You can spend money till you're black in the face. Mirandolina simply doesn't regard you.

CONTE: Nor does she you, for all your great nobility. It's money these people want.

MARCHESE: Money? Rubbish! Protection. The ability to do a kindness as needed.

CONTE: The ability to lend a hundred florins as needed!

MARCHESE: One must be able to command respect.

CONTE: And money does so.

MARCHESE: You've no idea what you're talking about.

CONTE: A better idea than you.

CAVALIERE: [*Entering from his room*] A quarrel - friends?

CONTE: We were arguing a rather nice point.

MARCHESE: [*With irony*] The Count was arguing - with me! - about the importance of rank!

CONTE: I was not denying its importance, merely maintaining if you want to avoid inconvenience, money is essential.

CAVALIERE: Actually, my dear Marchese...

MARCHESE: Oh, really, can't we talk about something else?

CAVALIERE: But what sparked off such a argument?

CONTE: Oh, the most ridiculous reason in the world.

MARCHESE: Of course, the Conte must make everything ridiculous.

CONTE: The Marchese is in love with our landlady. I too, only more so. He claims his love is requited, as a tribute to his rank. I hope mine is, as a reward for my attention. Does that not seem ridiculous to you?

MARCHESE: It is necessary to realise the care with which I accord her my protection.

CONTE: He offers protection. I offer money.

CAVALIERE: It's hard to tell which of you is the less deserving! Argue over a woman? Upset yourselves over a woman? A woman?! I cannot believe my ears. A woman? There is certainly no danger of that happening to me. I have never liked women, never held them to be of any account, and always considered them to be an insufferable nuisance.

MARCHESE: However that may be, Mirandolina is a woman quite out of the ordinary.

CONTE: There the Marchese is right, for once.

MARCHESE: Of course I am. If I am in love with her, she must be quite - out of the ordinary.

CAVALIERE: This is beginning to amuse me. How is she so - out of the ordinary?

MARCHESE: She has a distinction that quite captivates one.

CONTE: Meaning she's pretty, talks well, dresses properly and has perfect taste.

CAVALIERE: None of that is worth twopence. I've been here for three days and that's not how she's struck me.

CONTE: Maybe you should take a closer look.

CAVALIERE: Oh, rubbish! I've seen all I want. She's a woman like any other.

MARCHESE: She is not like any other. I am, sir, used to the society of the finest ladies in the land, and never - never, sir - have I encountered a woman so able to combine modesty and charm.

CONTE: *Cospetto di Bacco*! I know my way around women: I am well aware of their shortcomings and weaknesses. But with this one, in spite of all my courtship and the expense I've been put to, I've not been able to so much as touch her hand.

CAVALIERE: Trickery! Consummate trickery! You poor innocents! You believe her, do you? Not me. Women? I give them all the widest berth I can.

CONTE: Have you never been in love?

CAVALIERE: No, nor shall I be. People have done their damnedest to marry me off, but I've never wanted to.

MARCHESE: But don't you want a son? to carry on your name?

CAVALIERE: I've often thought of that, but then I think to have a son, I'd have to suffer a wife, and the fancy passes, quite suddenly.

CONTE: But what will you do with your money?

CAVALIERE: Enjoy the little I have with my friends.

MARCHESE: Bravo, Cavaliere, bravo; we shall give you every assistance.

CONTE: And none of it will be going on women?

CAVALIERE: Not a penny.

CONTE: Here she is. Now tell me she isn't adorable!

CAVALIERE: Four times rather have a good hunting-dog.

MARCHESE: Well, if you don't appreciate her, I do. Quite out of the ordinary!

MIRANDOLINA: [*Entering*] Gentlemen! Which of you was it wished to see me?

MARCHESE: It was I. But not here.

MIRANDOLINA: Where would you like me, *Eccellenza*? [*The MARCHESE whispers to her*] In your room? If you need anything, be good enough to call the waiter.

MARCHESE: [*To CAVALIERE*] Modesty! Charm!

CAVALIERE: Impertinence!

CONTE: Mirandolina, I can speak to you in public rather than give you the inconvenience of coming to my room. Look at these ear-rings. Do you like them?

MIRANDOLINA: Beautiful.

CONTE: They are diamonds, I'd have you know.

MIRANDOLINA: Yes, I know what diamonds look like.

CONTE: And they are yours.

CAVALIERE: (My dear man, you're throwing them away)

MIRANDOLINA: But why are you giving them to me?

MARCHESE: What a splendid present! She has others twice as beautiful.

CONTE: These are set in the latest style. Please accept them with my love.

CAVALIERE: (What a lunatic!)

MIRANDOLINA: Ah, now, really, signore...

CONTE: If you do not accept then, I shall be most put out.

MIRANDOLINA: I don't know what to say... I am at pains to keep the good-will of my guests... I would not want to put you out, Conte... I accept them!

CAVALIERE: (What a devil!)

CONTE: [*To CAVALIERE*] (Devilish obliging, don't you think?)

CAVALIERE: (I do indeed! She'll eat you up, spit you out and never a word of thanks!)

MARCHESE: Really, Conte, you surpass yourself, giving presents to a lady in public! Just to show off! Mirandolina, I need to speak to you in private, strictly *tête-à-tête*. Word of a gentleman.

MIRANDOLINA: (And nothing in it for me!) If that is all, I shall withdraw.

CAVALIERE: A moment, mistress. I'm not satisfied with the sheets in my room; if you have no better, perhaps I should provide my own.

MIRANDOLINA: Yes, signore, I have better. I shall see you get them - though I think you might have brought the matter up a little more politely.

CAVALIERE: I'm paying good money. Do I have to pay compliments as well?

CONTE: [*To MIRANDOLINA*] Be patient with him. A sworn enemy to womankind.

CAVALIERE: And I have no need of your support, thank you.

MIRANDOLINA: Poor women! What did they do to you? Why so cruel with us, Cavaliere?

CAVALIERE: Enough of that. There is no need for familiarity. Just change my sheets. I'll send my man for them. Gentlemen, your servant. [*He goes out*]

MIRANDOLINA: What a bear. I never saw anything like it !

CONTE: Ah, Mirandolina, it is not everyone who can recognise your qualities.

MIRANDOLINA: No, really, his behaviour has upset me so much I shall ask him to look for lodgings elsewhere.

MARCHESE: Yes, indeed, and if he makes any fuss about leaving, tell me, and I'll send him packing on the spot. Make use of my protection.

CONTE: [*Together with the MARCHESE*] And don't you worry about losing money, I'll make up for it, pay everything. (Listen, if you send the Marchese away too, I'll pay for him as well!)

MIRANDOLINA: Thank you, gentlemen, thank you. I think I have spirit enough to tell a guest I don't want him, and as for money, I never have an empty room for long.

FABRIZIO: [*Entering, to the CONTE*] *Illustrissimo*, someone is asking for you.

CONTE: D'you know who it is?

FABRIZIO: I think it is a jeweller. (Have some sense, Mirandolina, this is no company for you) [*He goes out*]

CONTE: Ah, yes, to show me a jewel. Mirandolina, a companion for the ear-rings.

MIRANDOLINA: Ah, signor Conte, no...

CONTE: You deserve the best, and money is no object - to me. I must go and have a look at this jewel. Goodbye - Mirandolina - Marchese, your servant. [*He goes out*]

MIRANDOLINA: Really, the signor Conte puts himself to too much trouble...

MARCHESE: Some people, if they have sixpence in the world, have to spend it on vanity, show. I know people like that, I know the way of the world.

MIRANDOLINA: So have I.

MARCHESE: They think women of your sort can be had for a few cheap presents.

MIRANDOLINA: Presents never did me any harm.

MARCHESE: I would think it an insult - giving you presents in order to place you under an obligation.

MIRANDOLINA: Oh, but the signor Marchese has never insulted me in that way!

MARCHESE: And I would never do so!

MIRANDOLINA: I am quite sure of that.

MARCHESE: But in any other way, command me.

MIRANDOLINA: I would need to know how?

MARCHESE: Anything. Make use of me.

MIRANDOLINA: But for goodness' sake, how?

MARCHESE: By Heavens! You have amazing qualities!

MIRANDOLINA: That is too gracious, *Eccellenza*.

MARCHESE: Ah! I could almost commit an imprudence. Almost curse my title.

MIRANDOLINA: Why is that, *Eccellenza*?

MARCHESE: I sometimes wish I were in the Count's position.

MIRANDOLINA: Because of his money?

MARCHESE: Eh? Money! A fig for it! No, if I were just a piddling little Count like him, I'd ...

MIRANDOLINA: You'd what?

MARCHESE: Damn it... I'd marry you! [*He goes out*]

MIRANDOLINA: [*Alone*] A fine thing, indeed! The Eccellentissimo Signor Marchese Church mouse would marry me! There's just one little difficulty - I wouldn't marry him! I like the roast, but what can one do with just the smell of cooking? It's putting to sea just to make oneself sick. If I had married all who said they wanted me, I'd have more husbands than the Grand Turk has wives. They all come to the hotel, fall in love with me, and most of them make pretence to marry me on the spot. And now this Signor Cavaliere treats me thus briskly? I don't say every man has to faint dead away at first sight of me, but to disprize me like that? It sticks in my gorge like a fishbone. Sworn enemy to women! Odious enmity! Cannot bear to look at them? Poor clown! He hasn't yet found the one who will manage him. But he will. He will. Maybe he has. Those who run after me are soon as tedious as a twice-told tale. Nobility is - the same as no nobility. Money is - money!

No less, but certainly no more. My whole delight is to see myself obliged, indulged, adored, and if that is my weakness, it is one I share with every woman born. As for marriage, I don't think of it: I have need of no one: I live honestly: I enjoy my freedom: and I shall make a butt of these affected travesties of desperate, moping lovers. And...
"I shall use every art of mind and feature
To bring to nought each priggish, barbarous creature
That scorns our sex, the noblest work of Nature!"

FABRIZIO: [*Enters*] *Ehi, padrona!*

MIRANDOLINA: What is it?

FABRIZIO: The guest in the middle room, complaining about the sheets.

MIRANDOLINA: I know, I know. He complained to me too. See to it.

FABRIZIO: Good. Can you come and put out the stuff for me to take up?

MIRANDOLINA: No, you run along. I'll take it myself.

FABRIZIO: You?

MIRANDOLINA: Yes, me.

FABRIZIO: He must have made an impression on you.

MIRANDOLINA: No more than anyone else. Get along with you.

FABRIZIO: (I knew it!)

MIRANDOLINA: (Poor boy!)

FABRIZIO: (She's only been leading me on)

MIRANDOLINA: (Him too)

FABRIZIO: (Just flattering me. Nothing'll come of it)

MIRANDOLINA: (I don't want to dash his hopes completely; he's a good servant)

FABRIZIO: It's always been agreed I wait on the guests.

MIRANDOLINA: You can be a little too off-hand with them.

FABRIZIO: And you can be a good deal too on-hand with them.

MIRANDOLINA: I know what I'm doing. I don't need lectures.

FABRIZIO: All right then. Find yourself another waiter.

MIRANDOLINA: What is the matter, Fabrizio? Are you angry with me?

FABRIZIO: You remember what your father said to the pair of us, before he died?

MIRANDOLINA: Yes: and when I want to get married, I shall remember what my father said.

FABRIZIO: It's just I'm a bit thin-skinned; there are some things I cannot stand.

MIRANDOLINA: But what do you think I am? A flirt? A nitwit? I'm surprised at you. How am I supposed to behave with guests who come and go like that? If I treat them well, I do it in my own interest, for the hotel. I don't need presents. I only need one to make love to: and him I have already. And I know what he deserves and I know the one who's right for me. And when I want to get married... I shall remember my father. And whoever has served me well won't regret it. I am grateful. I know who deserves a reward... but he doesn't know me. There, Fabrizio, try to understand me. If you can.

[*she goes out*]

FABRIZIO: It'll take a cleverer man than I am to understand her. One minute it seems she wants me, the next she doesn't. She says she isn't a flirt, she just seems to want to act like one. I don't know what to say. Wait and see. I like her, I love her, we've a lot in common, I'd gladly throw in with her for the rest of my life. Best turn a blind eye, and let things take their course. In the end guests come and go. I'm always here, like the poor. I'll always win in the end.

[*He goes out*]

# SCENE 2

The CAVALIERE's room

STEFANO: *Illustrissimo*, this letter arrived for you.

CAVALIERE: Bring me my chocolate. [*STEFANO goes out. The CAVALIERE opens the letter and reads*] "Siena, January the first, 1753" - who's this from? Ah, Orazio Taccagni - "My very dear friend, the tender friendship I have for you urges me to tell you your return home is imperative. Count Manna is dead... " - poor Manna, I'm sorry to hear it - "He has left an only daughter of marriageable age and heiress to one hundred and fifty thousand pounds. All your friends are anxious to see such a fortune fall to you ,and are making arrangements..." They needn't trouble themselves, they all know perfectly well I wouldn't give a woman house-room. And this dear friend, who knows me best, pesters me most. [*He tears up the letter*] What are a hundred and fifty thousand pounds to me? As a bachelor I can live well on half as much: as a husband I'd barely survive on twice as much. Take a wife? I'd sooner take a purge.

MARCHESE: *Amico*, may I join you?

CAVALIERE: The honour is mine.

MARCHESE: Yes, indeed, we speak the same language: that oaf of a Conte is not worthy to converse with us.

CAVALIERE: Marchese, forgive me; one should respect others if one wants to be respected oneself.

MARCHESE: Come now, you know me. Courteous to all the world, only I can't abide that fellow.

CAVALIERE: Because he is your rival in love? Shame on you! A nobleman of your standing in love with a landlady? A man of the world like you?

MARCHESE: I am bewitched!

CAVALIERE: This is madness! What witchcraft? Why is it I am not bewitched? Because I keep my distance from them, and run no risk of infection.

MARCHESE: You could be right. And then again... wrong. What preoccupies me at the minute is my factor in the country.

CAVALIERE: He's cheating you?

[*STEFANO brings on a single cup of chocolate*]

MARCHESE: Words fail me. Ah, chocolate!

CAVALIERE: [*To STEFANO*] Bring another cup.

STEFANO: They've run out.

CAVALIERE: Then they'd better run out and get some more. Please, Marchese...

MARCHESE: [*Takes the chocolate without ceremony, drinking and talking at the same time*] As I was saying, my factor... He'd promised to send me... Twenty guineas...

CAVALIERE: (Here it comes)

MARCHESE: And he hasn't.

CAVALIERE: A slight delay?

MARCHESE: No, but the point... the point... There. [*Gives the cup to STEFANO*] The point is I'm a good bit in debt, and don't know where to turn.

CAVALIERE: A week more or less...

MARCHESE: But, as a man of quality, you will know the importance of keeping one's word. I find myself in debt, and... it's enough to make one want to have a go at Providence!

CAVALIERE: I'm sorry to see you so discomposed. (How do I get out of this with credit?)

MARCHESE: Would it be so very difficult for you... A week merely... or two...

CAVALIERE: Marchese, *caro*, if I could, I would, with pleasure. I am waiting for funds myself.

MARCHESE: You're not trying to tell me you have no money!

CAVALIERE: There. There is my entire fortune. Doesn't add up to two guineas. [*Puts money on the table*]

MARCHESE: But that is a whole guinea.

CAVALIERE: My last.

MARCHESE: Lend me that. In the meantime, I'll see...

CAVALIERE: But what am I...

MARCHESE: What are you afraid of? I shall pay it back.

CAVALIERE: There's nothing more to be said, then. Help yourself.

MARCHESE: Pressing business... *amico*: much obliged for the moment: we shall meet at supper. [*Takes the guinea and leaves*]

CAVALIERE: [*Alone*] There's good work! He wanted to fleece me of twenty guineas, and was glad to get away with one. Well - one guinea makes no great difference either way, and if he doesn't pay it back, he won't come scrounging for more. What does irritate me, is he drank my chocolate - manners of a dancing-master! But then - I am a person of standing! I'd give him standing. Wouldn't be able to sit down for a week.

MIRANDOLINA: [*Enters with the sheets*] May I, *Illustrissimo*?

CAVALIERE: [*Brusque*] What is it?

MIRANDOLINA: Here is some better linen.

CAVALIERE: Good. Put it over there.

MIRANDOLINA: May I beg you to trouble yourself to see whether it is up to your standards?

CAVALIERE: What's it made of?

MIRANDOLINA: Cambric.

CAVALIERE: Cambric?

MIRANDOLINA: Ten shillings a yard, signore.

CAVALIERE: All I was wanting was something better than I had been given.

MIRANDOLINA: I made this for persons of standing, people who can recognise and appreciate such things; I wouldn't give them to every-body, *Illustrissimo*.

CAVALIERE: (Persons of standing! The usual flattery!)

MIRANDOLINA: Have you looked at this table-cloth?

CAVALIERE: But that is Flanders cloth, it gets ruined in the wash, there's no need to dirty it for me.

MIRANDOLINA: Serving a person of such... standing, I never bother with trifles. I have several of these, and will keep them aside for you, *Eccellenza, Illustrissimo*.

CAVALIERE: (One can't deny, she's a very obliging woman)

MIRANDOLINA: (He really seems determined to dislike women)

CAVALIERE: Give the linen to my servant, or put it down there. There's no need for you to put yourself out.

MIRANDOLINA: It's no bother, for a person of such...

CAVALIERE: Yes, yes, that will be all. (The creature wants to lay it on thick. They're all the same)

MIRANDOLINA: I'll put it in the cupboard.

CAVALIERE: Where you like.

MIRANDOLINA: [*Putting the linen in the cupboard*] (A ten-minute egg, I'm afraid I'll get nowhere)

CAVALIERE: (Fools start by listening to these fine phrases, and end up believing them)

MIRANDOLINA: Now then, what would you like for dinner?

CAVALIERE: Whatever you have.

MIRANDOLINA: But I must know what you like. If there's anything you like specially, you must tell me.

CAVALIERE: If I want anything, I shall tell my servant.

MIRANDOLINA: But men don't pay such attention to these things as women. A nice ragout perhaps, or something highly-spiced, please, you must tell me.

CAVALIERE: Thank you; but you're not dealing with the Conte or the Marchese now..

MIRANDOLINA: Ah! Did you ever see such a pair of Willy Wetlegs! They come to stay at my hotel and then pretend to be desperately in love with the owner! As if I had nothing better to do than pay mind to their nonsense. For the good of the house, I exchange a few pleasant words with them, but when I see them flattering themselves, I can't help laughing.

CAVALIERE: I like your frankness.

MIRANDOLINA: If I have one good quality, it's frankness.

CAVALIERE: But you are quite capable of treating your suitors with something less.

MIRANDOLINA: Me? Heaven forfend! Ask them whether I ever gave them a single sign of affection, or behaved in any way that would give them grounds to flatter themselves. Rebuff them? No, not quite, that would not be in my own interests, I don't go that far, but very nearly. I can't abide the sight of such affected men, any more than I can that of women who run after men. I'm not a schoolgirl any more. I'm getting on: and I'm not beautiful, though I have had my share of opportunities; but I've never wanted to get married, I value my freedom too much.

CAVALIERE: Yes, freedom's a great treasure.

MIRANDOLINA: And so many people just throw it away.

CAVALIERE: I know what I am doing, though... Keep your distance!

MIRANDOLINA: Does *Illustrissimo* have a wife?

CAVALIERE: *Illustrissimo* most certainly does not, Heaven forbid.

MIRANDOLINA: Excellent. Stay like that! Women, signore... well, it's not my place to speak ill of my own sex.

CAVALIERE: Well, you're the first woman I've ever heard talk like this.

MIRANDOLINA: Let me tell you something: innkeepers hear and see a lot of things; and I really sympathise with men who are afraid of our sex.

CAVALIERE: (She is an unusual woman!)

MIRANDOLINA: [*Making to go*] With your permission, signore...?

CAVALIERE: Oh, must you go?

MIRANDOLINA: I don't want to be a nuisance.

CAVALIERE: Not at all.

MIRANDOLINA: You see, Signore? It's just how I am with the others. I spend a moment or two with them, I'm friendly by nature, I pass a few pleasantries to amuse them, and *hop*! Suddenly they imagine they're terribly in love with me.

CAVALIERE: Because you have nice manners.

MIRANDOLINA: [*With a curtsey*] Too kind, *Illustrissimo*.

CAVALIERE: And they really fall in love?

MIRANDOLINA: Think of it - too ridiculous! Falling in love with a woman, just like that!

CAVALIERE: I've never been able to understand it.

MIRANDOLINA: How strong-minded you are! How manly!

CAVALIERE: Weakness! Poor wretched creatures!

MIRANDOLINA: There speaks a real man! Signor Cavaliere, give me your hand!

CAVALIERE: My hand? What for?

MIRANDOLINA: No, please; look, mine is quite clean.

CAVALIERE: There.

MIRANDOLINA: This is the first time I've had the honour of shaking hands with a man who thinks like a man.

CAVALIERE: Yes - well - that's enough.

MIRANDOLINA: Why, if I'd taken the hand of either of those other two sillies, they'd have fainted dead away. I wouldn't allow them the slightest liberty with me, not for all the tea in China. They don't understand how to behave. It's so wonderful to be able to converse freely, without all those... *Illustrissimo*, forgive my forwardness. Anything I can do for you, you have only to ask, I shall give you attention I have never given anyone else in the world.

CAVALIERE: And what is the reason for such partiality?

MIRANDOLINA: Because - apart from what you deserve, apart from your rank - I am sure I can behave naturally with you, without being afraid you would ever abuse my attention, and that you will always think of me as a servant, and not pester me with a lot of silly affectation.

CAVALIERE: (What is it makes her so out of the ordinary?)

MIRANDOLINA: (He's coming round)

CAVALIERE: (I don't understand)

MIRANDOLINA: (Bit by bit)

CAVALIERE: Well, then, if you've things to get on with, don't let me detain you.

MIRANDOLINA: Yes, signore, I must go about my little household duties. They are my real grand passion. If there's anything you want, I'll send the waiter.

CAVALIERE: Good... if you put in an appearance yourself from time to time, I shall be delighted to see you.

MIRANDOLINA: I never enter the guests' rooms... but I can make an exception for you, from time to time.

CAVALIERE: Why for me?

MIRANDOLINA: Because, signore, I like you very much.

CAVALIERE: You do?

MIRANDOLINA: I do. You're not affected, and you don't fall in love. (If you haven't done so by tomorrow, I'll eat my hat!) [*she goes out*]

CAVALIERE: [*Alone*] Oh, I know what I'm about. Women? Not with a ten-foot pole! This one might possibly ensnare me sooner than many. Than any? That candour, that frankness of utterance is a thing uncommon. She has something quite - out of the ordinary; but I'll not let go of my heart for all that. For a little divertissement, I'd sooner her company than another's. But love? No danger of that. Madmen, madmen all, that toil and moil after such finical, egotistical creatures.

"In deepest dungeons I'll my body bind
Sooner than lay in chains my freeborn mind.
Who trusts a villain loses but his purse,
Who trusts a woman loses much, much worse.
A biting flea we scratch where'er it itches;
But women leave us nothing in our breeches."

# SCENE 3

FABRIZIO: If your ladyships would care to inspect the other rooms...

ORTENSIA: These will suit very well, my man. Are you the proprietor or the waiter?

FABRIZIO: The waiter, at your ladyships' service.

DEJANIRA: (Ladyships indeed!)

ORTENSIA: (We should favour the deceit, dearest) Waiter!

FABRIZIO: Your ladyship?

ORTENSIA: Tell the landlord I wish to discuss the accommodation with him.

FABRIZIO: [*Going out*] The landlady will be here at once. (What the devil are these two doing here? Unaccompanied? By their airs and manner they would seem to be ladies)

DEJANIRA: He took us for ladies.

ORTENSIA: Good. We shall be the better accommodated.

DEJANIRA: But won't we have to pay more?

ORTENSIA: Oh, for the bills, leave me alone for that. I wasn't born yesterday.

DEJANIRA: I would not have these titles bring us into any difficulties.

ORTENSIA: *Cara*, you are frumpish and poor-spirited. Two actresses of talent and experience, accustomed as we are to portraying countesses, marchionesses, princesses upon the public stage, and shall we have difficulty sustaining such a character at a mere inn?

DEJANIRA: But when the rest of the company joins us...

ORTENSIA: They shall not join us yet awhile. From Pisa to Florence by boat will take them at least three days.

DEJANIRA: Bless me, how brutish! Travelling by boat!

ORTENSIA: A sad lack of funds. We were well nigh beggared coming by coach.

DEJANIRA: A piece of good fortune obtaining that further engagement.

ORTENSIA: Indeed and indeed, but if I did not busy myself with everything, nothing would ever be done.

FABRIZIO: [*Entering*] The mistress will be with your ladyships straight away.

ORTENSIA: Good.

FABRIZIO: And I would be glad for your ladyships to make good use of me. I have served many other ladies, and it would be an honour to give satisfaction to your ladyships.

ORTENSIA: We shall summon you at need.

DEJANIRA: (Oh, Ortensia, you did that beautifully!)

FABRIZIO: [*Takes out a pen and paper*] Meantime, if I might beg your ladyships to favour me with your names and addresses? For the Police.

DEJANIRA: Heavens!

ORTENSIA: And why, pray, should I give you my name?

FABRIZIO: We are obliged to report the name, address, birthplace, and condition of all travellers staying at the hotel. If we don't then woe betide us.

DEJANIRA: (*Amica*, 'tis farewell to our nobility)

ORTENSIA: Many doubtless give false names.

FABRIZIO: In which case we write down the name they give us, and look no further.

ORTENSIA: Then write - the Baronessa Ortensia del Poggio, from Palermo.

FABRIZIO: [*Writing it down*] (Sicilian, eh? And hot as mustard, I'll be bound) And you ladyship?

DEJANIRA: I? (I don't know what to say)

ORTENSIA: Come, come, Countess Dejanira, give the fellow your name.

FABRIZIO: If you please...

DEJANIRA: Didn't you hear it?

FABRIZIO: Her Excellency the Countess Dejanira... and the surname?

DEJANIRA: You want that as well?

ORTENSIA: Yes, del Sole, from Rome.

FABRIZIO: That is all I require. Please excuse the inconvenience. (Didn't I say they were ladies? I hope I do well. Tips will not be wanting)
[*He goes out*]

DEJANIRA: I am your ladyship's most humble servant.

ORTENSIA: Contessa, yours.

DEJANIRA: "What happy stroke of fortune doth me grant
            This happier chance of paying my respect?"

ORTENSIA: "Forth from the fountain of your generous heart
            Gush torrents pure, compound of grace sublime."

DEJANIRA: "You flatter me, Contessa."

ORTENSIA:                                Say not so!
            Your merits are deserving twice my praise."

MIRANDOLINA: [*Entering unnoticed*] Lord, what ceremonies!

DEJANIRA: I shall burst my stays!

ORTENSIA: Hush! The proprietress.

MIRANDOLINA: Ladies, your servant.

ORTENSIA: Good morning, gel.

DEJANIRA: Signora, your servant.

ORTENSIA: [*Warning DEJANIRA*] (Ehi!)

MIRANDOLINA: I humbly kiss your hands.

ORTENSIA: You're most obliging.

MIRANDOLINA: And your ladyship's.

DEJANIRA: Oh, no, really, it doesn't matter...

ORTENSIA: Come, come, let the wench show her good breedin'. Give her your hand.

MIRANDOLINA: So please you.

DEJANIRA: Here then.

MIRANDOLINA: Your ladyship laughs? At what?

ORTENSIA: Tush, the dear Contessa! She laughs still at me. I lately expressed a folly and it was that made her laugh.

MIRANDOLINA: (I'll be bound they are no ladies. Or they would hardly be travelling alone)

ORTENSIA: About our entertainment, if we might perhaps discuss...

MIRANDOLINA: But! You are alone! Have you no protection? no servants? nothing?

ORTENSIA: My husband, the Barone...

MIRANDOLINA: [*To DEJANIRA*] Why do you laugh, signora?

ORTENSIA: Yes, why do you laugh?

DEJANIRA: At your husband, the Barone!

ORTENSIA: Ah, yes, a mad wretch of a cavaliere: never one to pass up a jest. But you should see the Signor Conte, husband of the Contessa here. [*To DEJANIRA*] Come, come, Contessina, hold yourself some-what within the limits of decorum, if you please.

MIRANDOLINA: Ladies, if you please. We are alone, no one can hear us. Could it be that these names of Contessa, Baronessa...

DEJANIRA: Oh, come, what's the use?

ORTENSIA: Contessa! Contessa!

MIRANDOLINA: I think I guess at your ladyship's meaning.

DEJANIRA: Then you're very clever.

MIRANDOLINA: You would say: what is the use of pretending to be ladies, when we are perhaps less than such? Ah! Am I right?

DEJANIRA: How did you guess?

ORTENSIA: A mighty fine actress, I must say. Never could sustain a character.

DEJANIRA: I cannot act at all off stage.

ORTENSIA: And not much on.

MIRANDOLINA: Brava, Signora Baronessa; I admire your frankness.

ORTENSIA: Every so often we enjoy a frolic.

MIRANDOLINA: And I admire persons of spirit. Ladies, please make free of my hospitality - I would only ask, if any travellers of rank should arrive, to let me have the use of your room: I will find you something else very comfortable.

DEJANIRA: Of course.

ORTENSIA: When I spend money I mean to be treated like a lady, and not be shunted from pillar to post like a chess-man.

MIRANDOLINA: Come, Baronessa, oblige me in this... Oh, there is a gentleman staying at the hotel. The mere sight of a woman will lure him.

ORTENSIA: Is he rich?

MIRANDOLINA: That I cannot say.

MARCHESE: [*Entering*] Do I intrude?

ORTENSIA: Out of all question.

MARCHESE: I am your ladyships' servant.

DEJANIRA: Sir, your most humble.

MARCHESE: [*To MIRANDOLINA*] Guests?

MIRANDOLINA: Yes, *Eccellenza*.

ORTENSIA: Mercy me! *Eccellenza*!

DEJANIRA: (Ortensia wants him for herself already)

MARCHESE: But who are these ladies?

MIRANDOLINA: This is the Baronessa Ortensia del Poggio, and this the Contessa Dejanira del Sole.

MARCHESE: Ladies, I swoon.

ORTENSIA: And your own name, Signore?

MARCHESE: I am the Marchese di Forlipopoli.

ORTENSIA: An honour to be acquainted with so perfect a gentleman.

MARCHESE: If I may serve, command.

ORTENSIA: We shall make use of your good offices, at need.

MARCHESE: You too, Contessa, I am your most faithful dog.

DEJANIRA: I should count myself only too happy, were I to have the honour to be cast in the role of your most humble handmaiden.

MIRANDOLINA: (Theatrically put)

ORTENSIA: (Good on the red blood - hopeless on the blue)

[*The MARCHESE: produces a silk handkerchief, unfolds it and makes a pretence of mopping his brow*]

MIRANDOLINA: That's a pretty handkerchief!

MARCHESE: Did you ever see such lace?

ORTENSIA: Superb. I never saw the like.

MARCHESE: From London, you know.

DEJANIRA: Really? It's very nice.

MARCHESE: The Conte, alas, throws his money away on trumpery. I suppose taste cannot be learnt.

MIRANDOLINA: The Signor Marchese is a man of knowledge, distinction and understanding.

MARCHESE: It must be folded properly, so it does not crease. Quality demands respect.

MIRANDOLINA: Shall I have it put in your room?

MARCHESE: No, in yours.

MIRANDOLINA: In mine - why?

MARCHESE: I'm giving it to you.

MIRANDOLINA: Oh, no, really, *Eccellenza*.

MARCHESE: Not another syllable. It is yours.

MIRANDOLINA: But I couldn't...

MARCHESE: Don't put me in a passion now!

MIRANDOLINA: Your Excellency knows I don't like to offend a soul. Well... So that you won't be angry... I accept.

DEJANIRA: [*To ORTENSIA*] (Oh, that was clever)

ORTENSIA: (A real loss to the green-room)

DEJANIRA: Signor Marchese, can one find such handkerchiefs in Florence? I should love to possess one just like it.

MARCHESE: That might be difficult - one can but try.

MIRANDOLINA: (*Brava Contessina!*)

ORTENSIA: *Caro* Marchese, perhaps we may have the honour of your company for a while?

DEJANIRA: Perhaps you could take dinner with us?

MARCHESE: Delighted! (Hush, Mirandolina, do not be jealous, you know I am yours and yours alone)

MIRANDOLINA: (Get along, I am glad to see you enjoying yourself)

ORTENSIA: You shall be our cicerone.

DEJANIRA: We know no one; no one here but you.

MARCHESE: Oh, dearest ladies, with all my heart.

CONTE: [*Enters*] Mirandolina, I was looking for you.

MIRANDOLINA: I am here with these ladies.

CONTE: Ladies? Your most obedient.

ORTENSIA: Your most devoted. (More feathers on this bird than the other)

DEJANIRA: (But I'm so bad at plucking)

MARCHESE: Ehi! Show the Count your handkerchief.

MIRANDOLINA: Signor Conte, look, see what a fine present the Marchese has made me.

CONTE: Delighted. Congratulations, Marchese.

MARCHESE: It's nothing, nothing at all. A toy, the merest trifle. Put it away now, Mirandolina, I'd rather you didn't show it off to people - I don't want every purse-proud little counter-jumper knowing my business.

CONTE: With these ladies' permission, I would desire a word with you.

ORTENSIA: Take your freedom, Sir.

MARCHESE: The handkerchief will get all creased in your pocket like that.

MIRANDOLINA: I shall wrap it in cotton wool.

CONTE: Observe this meagre diamond.

MIRANDOLINA: Oh, how beautiful!

MARCHESE: (Damn the man! and damn his diamonds and his money! And whatever devil possesses him!)

CONTE: It would set off the ear-rings I gave you. It is yours.

MIRANDOLINA: But I simply cannot accept it.

CONTE: Now, now, don't make me angry!

MIRANDOLINA: *Eccellenza* knows I don't like to offend a soul. Well, so that you won't be angry, I'll accept. What do you say, Marchese? Is it not a fine stone?

MARCHESE: The handkerchief is far, far finer. Of its kind.

CONTE: Somewhat of a difference in kind, I'd say.

MARCHESE: At it again! Boasting of extravagance in public.

CONTE: Ah, yes, we know you display your gifts in secret.

ORTENSIA: Who might this other gentleman be?

CONTE: The Conte di Albafiorita, at your service.

DEJANIRA: (Lord! It's a famous family. I've heard the name)

ORTENSIA: Are you staying here?

CONTE: I am.

DEJANIRA: Do you entertain much?

CONTE: One could say so.

MARCHESE: Ladies, you must be tired of standing all this while. Permit me to wait upon you in your rooms.

ORTENSIA: We are infinitely obliged to you, sir. Signor Conte, what part of the country do you hail from?

CONTE: Naples.

ORTENSIA: Ah, then we are almost compatriots, almost neighbours. I am from... Palermo.

DEJANIRA: I am from Rome, but I have been to Naples, and it has always been my greatest curiosity to speak with a Neapolitan nobleman.

CONTE: But, Madama, are you alone? Have you no men with you?

MARCHESE: I am with these ladies, sir, they have no need of you.

ORTENSIA: We are alone, signor Conte.

CONTE: Mirandolina!

MIRANDOLINA: Signor Conte?

CONTE: Prepare my room for three. Would you deign to do me this favour?

ORTENSIA: We are stunned by your good breedin'.

MARCHESE: But I have been invited by these ladies...

CONTE: They are their own mistresses, to be sure. I would only say that at my poor table, there is no room for more than three.

MARCHESE: But I wanted to...

ORTENSIA: Let us go, Conte. The Marchese will honour us another time.

DEJANIRA: Signor Marchese, should you find the twin to that handkerchief, I should be more than grateful.

[*They go out*]

MARCHESE: (Albafiorita, you will pay for this!)

CONTE: What is the matter?

MARCHESE: I am a man of standing, and I'll not be treated thus. *Basta...* which of them is it desires a handkerchief? Ha! She can whistle for it. Mirandolina, take good care of it. Handkerchiefs of that quality do not grow on trees. Diamonds maybe, handkerchiefs - never!

[*He goes out*]

MIRANDOLINA: Poor silly man!

CONTE: Mirandolina - dearest - let it not displease you that I accompany these two ladies.

MIRANDOLINA: Not in the very least, signore.

CONTE: I do it for you. To increase the custom of the hotel. I am yours. My heart is yours. My fortune is yours. Dispose of them as you will. I make you mistress of all.

ORTENSIA: [*Off*] Signor Conte! [*He hurries out*]

MIRANDOLINA: [*Alone*] Go! With all his money and all his presents, he will never get me to be in love with him; and a lot less with the Marchese and his ridiculous airs and graces. I am about to engage with the Cavaliere di Ripafratta, and I would not give over such a pleasure for a jewel of twice the value. I shall make assay: I do not know whether I have the capabilities of our two impudent players there, but I shall make assay. Is it possible he should not yield? No - who can resist a woman if she takes time and trouble to employ her art?

"He needs fear no pursuit who flies the field,
But he who stands must to a woman yield."

□

# ACT TWO

## SCENE 1

The CAVALIERE 's room

FABRIZIO: Tell your master the soup's ready if he is.

STEFANO: You tell him.

FABRIZIO: I don't speak to him unless I have to.

STEFANO: His bark is worse than his bite. He can't bear women, but he's all right with men. Sweetness itself.

FABRIZIO: (Can't bear women? Poor fool! Doesn't know what's good for him. Or does he?) [*He goes out*]

STEFANO: *Illustrissimo* is served.

CAVALIERE: Earlier than usual. [*Starts eating. STEFANO stands behind his chair*]

STEFANO: This room gets served first of all. The Count of Albafiorita was bawling about he wanted to be first served, but the lady of the house said you were to be, signore.

CAVALIERE: Good of her.

STEFANO: A real lady, that one. I've met all sorts, but never a landlady like her.

CAVALIERE: [*Turning slightly to him*] Like her, do you?

STEFANO: If it weren't for leaving you, signore, I'd be happy to come and work for her as a waiter.

CAVALIERE: Poor fool! What do you think she'd do with you?

STEFANO: I'd follow a woman like that around like a little dog, signore. [*He goes for the next course*]

CAVALIERE: Good heavens, the woman seems to cast a spell on everyone! It would a joke if she cast one on me too. No, tomorrow I leave for Livorno - she can start busying herself today, if she can, but she had better realise I am no easy prey. It'll take more than her to overcome my aversion to women.

STEFANO: [*Entering with chicken and a dish*] The landlady says if you don't want the chicken, she can send up a pigeon.

CAVALIERE: I like anything. Well, what's that?

STEFANO: She specially asked to let her know if *Illustrissimo* liked the sauce, because she made it with her own hands.

CAVALIERE: More and more obliging. [*Tries it*] Delicious! Tell her I like it very much, and give her my compliments.

STEFANO: Yes, signore.

CAVALIERE: Do it now.

STEFANO: Yes, signore.

CAVALIERE: At once!

STEFANO: Yes, signore. (Incredible! Compliments to a woman!)
[*He goes out*]

CAVALIERE: The sauce is really delicious. Best I ever tasted. If this is how Mirandolina carries on, she won't want for guests. Good food, good linen - eventually. And one must admit, she is quite - out of the ordinary. Though what I admire most is her honesty: that is the great thing. Why do I dislike women? Because they are flatterers, cheats and liars. But honesty like that...

STEFANO: [*Coming back in*] she thanks *Illustrissimo* for his kindness in appreciation of her poor efforts.

CAVALIERE: Well done. That was a mouthful.

STEFANO: And she's making something else with her own hands, but I don't know what it is.

CAVALIERE: She is actually making it?

STEFANO: Yes, signore.

CAVALIERE: Get me a drink.

STEFANO: Yes, signore.

CAVALIERE: I shall have to find some way of paying her back for all this. She's too generous: I shall have to pay double. Pay her well and leave quickly. [*STEFANO: brings his drink*] Has the Count has his luncheon yet?

STEFANO: He has just been served, *Illustrissimo*. He is entertaining today - two ladies with him.

CAVALIERE: Who are they?

STEFANO: They arrived at the hotel a few hours back. I don't know who they are.

CAVALIERE: Does the Count know them?

STEFANO: I don't think he did: but the moment he clapped eyes on them, he asked them to lunch.

CAVALIERE: Idiot! Hardly seen them, and straight in head first! And they accept! Heaven knows who they are, but... they're women, and that is enough. The Count will ruin himself, that's clear. Tell me, what about the Marchese ?

STEFANO: He left the house, and no one's seen him since.

CAVALIERE: [*Pushing his plate aside*] Good. I'm ready.

STEFANO: Yes, signore.

CAVALIERE: Lunching with two women! Dear God! Enough to ruin a man's appetite.

MIRANDOLINA: [*Entering with a dish*] May I?

CAVALIERE: Who is it?

STEFANO: It's - it's your lunch, signore!

CAVALIERE: Relieve the dish of that lady... mm.

MIRANDOLINA: No, no, don't rob me of the pleasure of serving you with my own hands.

CAVALIERE: That's no sort of work for you.

MIRANDOLINA: Oh, signore, who am I? A lady? I am a servant whom you honour by staying at my hotel.

CAVALIERE: (Modesty, yes!)

MIRANDOLINA: To tell the truth, I would be happy to wait on all my guests, but there are certain considerations which forbid it, I don't know if you understand me. But I know I need have no doubts about you, signore.

CAVALIERE: Thank you. What have we here?

MIRANDOLINA: A ragout. I made it myself.

CAVALIERE: It will be delicious. If you made it, it will be delicious.

MIRANDOLINA: Oh, signore, now you are too kind. I don't do anything well; I wish I did, then I could really serve a gentleman of such standing.

CAVALIERE: (Livorno tomorrow!) If you've other things to do, don't let me keep you.

MIRANDOLINA: I have nothing to do, signore: the hotel is quite adequately staffed. I should just like to know if that is to your taste.

CAVALIERE: I shall try it. Couldn't be better! What a flavour! I can't quite place it.

MIRANDOLINA: I have my secrets, signore. There are some things these hands can do.

CAVALIERE: [*To STEFANO*] Get me another drink.

MIRANDOLINA: With that, signore, you should be drinking something especially good.

CAVALIERE: [*To STEFANO, with some heat*] Get me another drink!

MIRANDOLINA: In my opinion, the best wine with that would be a good Frascati.

CAVALIERE: The wine of my country! You are a good judge of everything, it would seem.

MIRANDOLINA: I don't make many mistakes.

CAVALIERE: Well, you have just made one.

MIRANDOLINA: In what, signore?

CAVALIERE: In thinking I deserve special attention. [*MIRANDOLINA sighs*] What's the matter? What was that sigh for?

MIRANDOLINA: Nothing, signore, nothing at all. No matter how much attention I pay everyone, it makes me sad to think they should be ungrateful.

CAVALIERE: I shall not be ungrateful to you.

MIRANDOLINA: Oh, I was not angling for thanks from you, I am simply doing my duty.

CAVALIERE: No, no - I know very well... I am not such a clumsy bear as you think me. I shall be no trouble to you. [*He pours wine*]

MIRANDOLINA: But, signore, I don't understand...

CAVALIERE: Your health!

MIRANDOLINA: Thank you. You do me too much honour.

CAVALIERE: This wine is excellent.

MIRANDOLINA: Frascati is one of my passions.

CAVALIERE: Will you have a glass?

MIRANDOLINA: Oh, thank you - no, signore.

CAVALIERE: Have you eaten?

MIRANDOLINA: Signore, yes.

CAVALIERE: You won't try a glass?

MIRANDOLINA: You are kinder than I deserve.

CAVALIERE: Not at all, my pleasure.

MIRANDOLINA: What can I say? Just a very little, then.

CAVALIERE: [*To STEFANO*] Bring another glass.

MIRANDOLINA: No, no, please, allow me, I will take this one.

CAVALIERE: But - but I've used that one.

MIRANDOLINA: [*Laughing*] Then I shall drink to your fine character. [*STEFANO puts the other glass on the tray*]

CAVALIERE: [*Pouring wine*] (The little hussy!)

MIRANDOLINA: I haven't eaten for some time: I hope it won't upset me.

CAVALIERE: No danger of that.

MIRANDOLINA: Perhaps if I could have a mouthful of bread?

CAVALIERE: Of course. Here... [*He gives her some bread. MIRANDOLINA, with the glass in one hand and the bread in the other, shows signs of unease*] But you're uncomfortable, won't you sit down?

MIRANDOLINA: Oh, no, that would be too much, signore.

CAVALIERE: Please, please, we're alone. [*To STEFANO*] Bring a chair.

STEFANO: (He must be sickening. I've never seen him this way)

MIRANDOLINA: Woe betide me if the Count or the Marchese knew about this.

CAVALIERE: Why?

MIRANDOLINA: A hundred times they've implored me eat and drink with them, but I never would.

CAVALIERE: Never mind, make yourself comfortable.

MIRANDOLINA: If you say so.

CAVALIERE: [*To STEFANO*] (And not a word about this to a living soul!)

STEFANO: Never fear. (Wonders will never cease)

MIRANDOLINA: [*Toasting*] To the Cavaliere! And everything that pleases him!

CAVALIERE: Thank you - you are a charming hostess.

MIRANDOLINA: That didn't include women.

CAVALIERE: What's that?

MIRANDOLINA: I know you can't stand the sight of them.

CAVALIERE: Quite true. I never could.

MIRANDOLINA: May you never change!

CAVALIERE: I wouldn't like... [*Looking at STEFANO*]

MIRANDOLINA: What wouldn't you like, signore?

CAVALIERE: Listen. [*Whispering to her*] (I wouldn't like you to change me in any way)

MIRANDOLINA: Me, signore? How would I do that?

CAVALIERE: [*To STEFANO*] Get out!

STEFANO: Do you want anything, signore?

CAVALIERE: Go and boil a couple of eggs. Bring them in when they're done.

STEFANO: Hard or soft, signore?

CAVALIERE: Like rocks.

STEFANO: (He's warming up)

CAVALIERE: Out!! [*STEFANO flees*] Mirandolina, you are a very delightful girl.

MIRANDOLINA: Oh, signore, you're making fun of me.

CAVALIERE: Listen. Let me tell you something true, absolutely true, something that redounds to your credit.

MIRANDOLINA: Oh, please tell me!

CAVALIERE: You are the very first woman I have ever, ever enjoyed talking to.

MIRANDOLINA: I don't know that that is so much to my credit, signore - there are times when temperaments just chime together, even with people who have never met before, a sort of sympathy, an affinity, a feeling. I myself, for instance, have a feeling for you I have never felt before. For anyone.

CAVALIERE: I fear you are trying to rob me of my peace of mind.

MIRANDOLINA: Oh, come, signore, you are a sensible man, do yourself justice. Don't give way to weakness like other people. If I thought you were going to do that, I wouldn't come here again. I too feel a... something... inside me, I never felt before; but I'm not going to lose my head over a man, certainly not one who hates women; one who - perhaps - perhaps - is leading me on, testing me, with a new way of talking, just to laugh at me later. Signor Cavaliere, may I have a little more wine?

CAVALIERE: What? Yes, of course... [*Pours wine*]

MIRANDOLINA: (He's ripe to drop)

CAVALIERE: There. [*Hands her the wine*]

MIRANDOLINA: Thank you. But aren't you drinking?

CAVALIERE: Yes, of course. (Better if I got drunk. One devil might chase out the other) [*Pours himself a glass*]

MIRANDOLINA: [*Exercising charm*] Signor Cavaliere.

CAVALIERE: What is it?

MIRANDOLINA: Touch glasses. To friendship.

CAVALIERE: Friendship!

MIRANDOLINA: To... those who feel for each other... to affinity... and no wicked thoughts...

CAVALIERE: Their health!

MARCHESE: [*Entering*] Here I am. Whose health are we drinking?

CAVALIERE: Was there something, Marchese?

MARCHESE: Forgive me, m'dear. I called and called but nobody came.

MIRANDOLINA: [*Making to go*] With your permission ---

CAVALIERE: Stay where you are. [*To MARCHESE*] I do not permit myself such liberties with you, signore.

MARCHESE: Pray forgive. Between old friends, I thought you were alone. But I am delighted to find you in the company of our charming hostess. Ah! What do you say? A masterpiece, is she not?

MIRANDOLINA: Signore, I was here to wait on the signor Cavaliere. I came over slightly faint, and he was good enough to give me a glass of wine to put me right.

MARCHESE: Would that be Frascati?

CAVALIERE: Yes.

MARCHESE: But real Frascati?

CAVALIERE: I'm paying the real price for it.

MARCHESE: I know about these things. Just let me try it, and I'll soon tell you whether it's real or not.

CAVALIERE: [*Calling*] Ehi! Bring a glass for the Marchese!

MARCHESE: Don't make it too small. Frascati's not a liqueur. To judge it properly you need a good swig.

STEFANO: [*Entering*] The eggs, signore.

MARCHESE: What's that you've got there?

CAVALIERE: Eggs.

MARCHESE: Take 'em away. Can't stand the things. [*STEFANO takes them away*]

MIRANDOLINA: Perhaps, Marchese, if the Cavaliere will permit, you would taste some of this ragout which I made, with my own hands.

MARCHESE: Yes, indeed. Here, you. A chair! [*STEFANO brings one*] A fork!

CAVALIERE: Set him a place.

MIRANDOLINA: Signor Cavaliere, I feel better. I shall go now.

MARCHESE: Do me the pleasure of staying a little longer.

MIRANDOLINA: But, signore, I have my work to attend to; and the signor Cavaliere...

MARCHESE: Do you mind if she stays a little longer?

CAVALIERE: What do you want with her?

MARCHESE: I want you both to try a little glass of Cyprus wine of mine, which I think you'll find quite unrivalled. I would particularly value Mirandolina's opinion of it.

CAVALIERE: Then you'd better stay. To please the Marchese.

MIRANDOLINA: The signor Marchese will forgive me.

MARCHESE: Don't you want to taste it?

MIRANDOLINA: Another time, *Eccellenza*.

CAVALIERE: Oh, come on, stay now.

MIRANDOLINA: Is that an order?

CAVALIERE: A request.

MIRANDOLINA: Then I obey it. [*Sits down again*]

CAVALIERE: (More obliging by the minute!)

MARCHESE: [*Eating*] Excellent! Quite superb! What a flavour!

CAVALIERE: [*To MIRANDOLINA*] (The Marchese is jealous of your sitting so close to me)

MIRANDOLINA: (He means nothing to me)

CAVALIERE: (You are a man-hater, then?)

MIRANDOLINA: (Just as you are a woman-hater)

CAVALIERE: (Is this how my enemies are to take their revenge on me?)

MIRANDOLINA: (What do you mean, signore?)

CAVALIERE: (You know quite well what I mean, signorina)

MARCHESE: My friend, your very good health!

CAVALIERE: Well? What do you think of it?

MARCHESE: With all respect, it's rubbish. Try my Cuprus wine.

CAVALIERE: But where is this Cyprus wine ?

MARCHESE: I have it by me. Carry it around with me. I want you to enjoy it. It's exquisite. There. [*Produces a minute bottle*]

MIRANDOLINA: From the look of it, Marchese, you don't want it going to our heads.

MARCHESE: This? You drink it by the drop, drop by drop. Glasses! [*STEFANO brings some*] Too large, too large! Have you no smaller?

CAVALIERE: Bring the liqueur glasses.

MIRANDOLINA: Perhaps we could just have a smell of it.

MARCHESE: [*Sniffing the bottle*] Beautiful! Most soothing! [*He goes through a rigmarole of pouring minute amounts into minute glasses, corking the bottle carefully*] Ah! Ambrosia! Nectar! Manna in the wilderness!

CAVALIERE: [To MIRANDOLINA] (What do you think of this rubbish?)

MIRANDOLINA: (Dregs!)

MARCHESE: Well? What do you say?

CAVALIERE: Good. Fine.

MARCHESE: Mirandolina?

MIRANDOLINA: Signore, I cannot pretend: I do not like it, I think it is horrible and I cannot say it is not. I admire people who can pretend and deceive. But those who can deceive in one thing can well deceive in another.

CAVALIERE: (That sounds like a hit at me. Though for the life of me, I can't think why)

MARCHESE: Mirandolina, you are clearly no judge of this sort of wine. I am sorry for you. You liked, you appreciated the handkerchief I gave you, but Cyprus wine is beyond your understanding.

MIRANDOLINA: [*To CAVALIERE, aside*] (Listen to the man!)

CAVALIERE: (I could never brag like that)

MIRANDOLINA: (You just brag about your dislike of women)

CAVALIERE: (And you about your overcoming men)

MIRANDOLINA: [*Coquettish*] (Not all men)

CAVALIERE: [*With some passion*] (Yes, all!)

MARCHESE: [*To STEFANO*] Here, you there, three clean glasses!

MIRANDOLINA: No more for me.

MARCHESE: No, no, have no fear, it's not for you. [*Pours Cyprus wine into the three new glasses STEFANO brings*] Now, my man, with your master's permission, go to the Count of Albafiorita, and tell him - loud enough for all to hear - tell him I beg him to try a little of my Cyprus wine.

STEFANO: Certainly, signore. (He won't be getting drunk off that) [*He goes*]

CAVALIERE: Marchese, you are too generous.

MARCHESE: I? Ask Mirandolina.

MIRANDOLINA: Oh, yes, indeed!

MARCHESE: Has the Cavaliere seen that handkerchief?

MIRANDOLINA: Not yet.

MARCHESE: Then show it him. [*To the CAVALIERE*] The flavour of this will be with me all evening. [*Puts the bottle, diminished by a thimbleful, back in his pocket*]

MIRANDOLINA: Make sure it doesn't do you any harm, Marchese.

MARCHESE: If you only knew what does do me harm!

MIRANDOLINA: What?

MARCHESE: Those beautiful eyes of yours!

MIRANDOLINA: Indeed?

MARCHESE: Cavaliere, I am desperately, irrevocably in love with her.

CAVALIERE: I'm sorry to hear it.

MARCHESE: You've never been in love with a woman. Oh, if you had been, you would sympathise with me.

CAVALIERE: Oh, I do, I do.

MARCHESE: It makes me bestially jealous. I let her sit close to you, because I know what you are; I wouldn't allow it with anyone else, not for a hundred thousand crowns.

CAVALIERE: (This is beginning to get on my nerves)

STEFANO: [*Entering with a bottle on a tray*] The signor Conte thanks *Eccellenza* and sends you this bottle of Canary.

MARCHESE: Oho! He thinks to put his miserable Canary on a level with my Cyprus! Let us see. Poor mad creature! Hogwash! Sheep dip! Tell from the smell.

CAVALIERE: Taste it first.

MARCHESE: I have no wish to taste it. This is a further impertinence on the part of the Count, to go with all the rest. Always trying to come over me. Provoke me. show me up. Make me do something beneath my dignity. Well, I swear, I shall do something to pay him back, a hundred fold. Mirandolina, if you don't turn him out of here, I shall do such things, what they are I know not, but... he's a... he's asking for it. I am a person of standing and I shall not stand for it.

[*Goes out, taking the bottle with him*]

CAVALIERE: The poor fellow's going mad.

MIRANDOLINA: At least he remembered to take the bottle with him, in case his rage overcomes him.

CAVALIERE: He's mad, I tell you. And you're the one to blame.

MIRANDOLINA: Am I the sort to drive men mad?

CAVALIERE: Yes, you are...

MIRANDOLINA: [*Getting up*] Signore, with your permission...

CAVALIERE: Stay where you are.

MIRANDOLINA: Forgive me; I make nobody go mad.

CAVALIERE: [*Getting up, but not leaving the table*] Listen to me.

MIRANDOLINA: [*Going*] Excuse me.

CAVALIERE: [*Commandingly*] I told you to stay where you are.

MIRANDOLINA: [*Turning haughtily*] Do you want something?

CAVALIERE: Nothing - [*Confused*] Let us have another glass of wine.

MIRANDOLINA: Well, let us be quick, I have to go.

CAVALIERE: Sit down.

MIRANDOLINA: I prefer standing. Standing!

CAVALIERE: [*Handing her a glass, gently*] Here then.

MIRANDOLINA: Let me give you a toast before I go. A little toast my grandmother taught me.
"Wine and Love are mighty powers:
Wine in our mouths, Love in our eyes,
And, before we realise,
Our poor hearts are no longer ours.
I drink the wine - and there's the cause
Why my eyes do the same as yours."

[*she laughs and goes out*]

CAVALIERE: Good! Now come here and listen to me... The little devil! She's escaped! Gone! And left a hundred other devils behind to torment me!

STEFANO: Shall I serve the dessert now?

CAVALIERE: Serve every man after his deserts and who shall escape whipping? Including you. Get out! [*STEFANO goes*] "... there's the cause why my eyes do the same as yours." What the devil is that supposed to mean? I know you, you little villain! You want to be the ruin, the death of me. But how gracefully, how fetchingly you do it... Damnation! Do you want to rub it in? I leave for Livorno tomorrow. Livorno? What am I saying? Samarkand! Trebizond! Peru! The moon! I shall never set eyes on her again. Where the devil is ashamed to go himself, he sends a woman. Damn all women - without women there would be no such thing as damnation.
"I swear, that I shall never, from this minute,
set foot within a house that has a woman in it!"

# SCENE 2
The CONTE's room

CONTE: The Marchese is a man of singular character. Nobly born, I grant you; but between his father and himself, they have wasted all their substance, and now he has barely enough to live. In spite of which it pleases him to act the fine gentleman.

ORTENSIA: One could well see his desire to please outran his means to do so.

DEJANIRA: What little he *does* give he requires the whole world to take note of.

CONTE: He would be a fine character for one of your comedies. You did well to discover yourselves to me. In this way I can do more to advantage you.

ORTENSIA: The Signor Conte is most generous with his protection.

CONTE: Your servant, where I can be, but there is a small consideration that prevents me from visiting your lodgings.

DEJANIRA: Whatever could it be?

ORTENSIA: Some little affinity of the heart?

CONTE: You have hit it. To a cow's thumb. Between ourselves, the proprietress of the hotel!

ORTENSIA: Mercy me! A great lady indeed! I wonder at you, Conte, to throw yourself away on an innkeeper!

DEJANIRA: It would be less shameful to lay out your charms to ensnare a comedienne.

CONTE: Making love to such as you, to tell the truth, affords me but scant satisfaction. Here today and gone tomorrow.

ORTENSIA: Is it not better thus, Signore? In this manner, friendships are not drawn out to an eternity, and gentlemen are not obliged to ruin themselves.

CONTE: Nevertheless, as things are, I am ensnared.

DEJANIRA: But what is so out of the ordinary with her?

CONTE: Ah, so many things!

ORTENSIA: Ehi, Dejanira, she is so pink and fresh.

DEJANIRA: She has a pretty wit.

ORTENSIA: Oh, now, for wit, would you set her up against us?

CONTE: Enough of this: be she as she may, Mirandolina pleases me, and as you value my friendship, speak well of her or we must be strangers once again.

ORTENSIA: Oh, Signore, for my part, Mirandolina is an Aphrodite.

DEJANIRA: Oh, yes, very aphrodisiac.

[*The CAVALIERE passes through the room*]

CONTE: That's more like it. Oh, did you see who just came through?

ORTENSIA: We did.

CONTE: Another good character for a play. He cannot abide the sight of a woman.

ORTENSIA: Oh! Oh! Pah! Filthy French beast!

DEJANIRA: Perhaps he has unhappy memories of one of our sex.

CONTE: Fiddlesticks! I doubt if he has any memories of them. Never been in love in his life, never wanted to be. Despises all women, and when I tell you he despises Mirandolina ...

ORTENSIA: Poor clown! If I were to put my mind to it, I'd wager I'd make him change his opinions.

DEJANIRA: The very idea! Despising women!

CONTE: Listen, friends. This is for pure diversion. If you should be successful in making him fall in love, I could promise you a fine present.

DEJANIRA: It was not in my mind to be rewarded; I do this for the frolic.

ORTENSIA: If the Signor Conte wishes to make himself agreeable, let him.

CONTE: I doubt you will make any headway in this.

ORTENSIA: Signor Conte, you have a small opinion of us.

DEJANIRA: Of course, we are hardly of the prodigious good breedin' of Mirandolina; but at the end of the day, we have some small experience of the world.

CONTE: Am I to send to him?

ORTENSIA: As you wish.

CONTE: Ehi! Is anybody there? [*FABRIZIO enters*] Inform the Cavaliere di Ripafratta I should count it a favour to speak with him.

FABRIZIO: He's not in his room.

CONTE: I just saw him going towards the kitchen. Find him.

FABRIZIO: At once. [*Goes out*]

CONTE: (Why was he going to the kitchen? Probably to tell Mirandolina off about her cooking)

ORTENSIA: Signor Conte, I asked the Marchese if he could recommend me a shoemaker, but I fear I shall see little of him now.

CONTE: Think no more of it. I shall recommend you to my own.

DEJANIRA: The Marchese promised me a handkerchief. But! Farewell it! *Hélas!*

CONTE: We shall find handkerchiefs enough.

DEJANIRA: They can be so necessary.

CONTE: [*Offering his own silk handkerchief*] If this will serve, please take it. It's quite clean.

DEJANIRA: La, sir, you overwhelm me with good breedin'.

CONTE: Ah, here is the Cavaliere. Sustain the characters of ladies of quality, so he may be the more compelled to be civil. Withdraw a little, to block any possible retreat.

ORTENSIA: What is his name?

CONTE: The Cavaliere di Ripafratta, in Tuscany.

DEJANIRA: Is he married?

CONTE: He cannot abide a woman.

ORTENSIA: Rich?

CONTE: Very.

DEJANIRA: Generous?

CONTE: Probably.

ORTENSIA: Come along!

DEJANIRA: I'm coming. [*They retire*]

CAVALIERE: Conte, you wished to see me?

CONTE: It was I gave you that inconvenience.

CAVALIERE: How may I be of service?

CONTE: These two ladies have need of you. [*They come forward*]

CAVALIERE: I beg to be excused. A... subsequent engagement.

ORTENSIA: Signore, in a word, you cast us off.

DEJANIRA: Rejected!

CAVALIERE: (Damn this Count!)

CONTE: *Caro* amico, a request from two ladies demands at least the civility of a hearing.

CAVALIERE: Your pardon. How may I be of service?

ORTENSIA: Are you not from Tuscany, signor?

CAVALIERE: That is correct.

DEJANIRA: Do you have friends in Florence?

CAVALIERE: And relations.

DEJANIRA: Let me explain, Signore... *cara*, perhaps you had better...

ORTENSIA: Let me say, Signor Cavaliere... you understand... a certain...

CAVALIERE: Signora, if you please, I have a pressing engagement.

CONTE: Ah, I understand - my presence renders them tongue-tied. Let me remove the cause of your uneasiness.

CAVALIERE: No, friend, don't go... please...

CONTE: [*Going out*] I know my duty. Your servant, ladies, signore.

ORTENSIA: You may take a seat, sir.

CAVALIERE: Thank you, I prefer standing.

DEJANIRA: Are you always this rustic before ladies?

CAVALIERE: Be so good as to tell me what you want of me.

ORTENSIA: Your assistance, your protection, your kindness.

CAVALIERE: What has befallen you?

ORTENSIA: Our husbands have abandoned us!

CAVALIERE: Abandoned? How? (Two abandoned women!) Who are your husbands?

DEJANIRA: [*To ORTENSIA*] Amica, don't get in too far.

CAVALIERE: Signora, I take my leave.

ORTENSIA: How, Sir? What manners are these?

DEJANIRA: A gentleman's? Hahaha.

CAVALIERE: Your pardon. I am a man of peace. I see before me two ladies abandoned by their husbands. That means a whole mountain of trouble, and I am not apt at trickeries. I keep myself to myself. Most honoured ladies, expect nothing from me in the way either of assistance or advice.

ORTENSIA: Oh, be off with you, then; let us not keep this amiable cavalier any longer in subjection.

DEJANIRA: Let us speak plainly to him.

CAVALIERE: What's this now?

ORTENSIA: We are not ladies.

CAVALIERE: No?

DEJANIRA: The Count wished to play a trick on you.

CAVALIERE: Then it is played. Good day to you.

ORTENSIA: Just a moment.

CAVALIERE: What do you want of me?

DEJANIRA: The pleasure of your company.

ORTENSIA: We shall not eat you.

DEJANIRA: Nor ruin your reputation. We know you cannot stand the sight of women.

CAVALIERE: Then you will appreciate that I take my leave.

ORTENSIA: Yet listen: we are not women who could cause you disappointment.

CAVALIERE: Then what are you?

ORTENSIA: Tell him, Dejanira.

DEJANIRA: You could tell him just as well.

CAVALIERE: Come along now, who the devil are you?

ORTENSIA: We are - actresses.

CAVALIERE: Oh, then, there is no need to be afraid. I have a great prejudice in favour of your art.

ORTENSIA: What do you mean?

CAVALIERE: I know you pretend onstage and off. Thus forewarned, I no longer fear you.

DEJANIRA: Signore, off the stage I have no skill at pretence.

CAVALIERE: What is your name, then? La Spuriosa?

DEJANIRA: I am...

CAVALIERE: [*To ORTENSIA*] And you, La Fraudulenta?

ORTENSIA: My good signore, I am here to tell you...

CAVALIERE: And I am here to tell you you're a couple of impertinent sluts.

DEJANIRA: Must I hear this?

ORTENSIA: This - to a woman of my condition?

CAVALIERE: Tell me, do you paint your face yourself - or must you summon the plasterer?

ORTENSIA: Painting, sir, how dare you?

CAVALIERE: That is a beautiful wig, one scarcely sees the join!

DEJANIRA: Impudent brute!

[*They leave*]

CAVALIERE: Well, I soon found how to get rid of them. What were they thinking of? To catch me in their toils? Poor silly creatures! Had they been ladies, I should have been obliged, from mere respect, to take to my heels. Still, when I can, I punish women with the greatest pleasure in the world. However, Mirandolina came over me with such a deal of civility, that I could find no way to punish her, indeed, I find myself almost obliged to be in love with her. I wish I was a thousand miles from here. And tomorrow I shall be. But can I wait till tomorrow? If I spend the night under this roof, who know whether Mirandolina may not accomplish her work of destruction? Yes! I shall act like a man! Ehi! Stefano!

STEFANO: Signore?

CAVALIERE: Get my bill.

STEFANO: The Marchese was waiting for you in his room. He would like a word with you.

CAVALIERE: What's that fatuous old relic after now? He'll be getting no more money from me, for sure. Let him wait, and when he's sick of that, he'll give up. Go and see to my bill at once.

STEFANO: Signore.

CAVALIERE: Wait! Have the luggage ready to leave in two hours.

STEFANO: We're leaving?

CAVALIERE: Yes. Bring my sword and hat, and don't say anything to the Marchese.

STEFANO: But what if he sees me with the luggage?

CAVALIERE: Improvise, man, improvise. Understand?

STEFANO: [Going] I don't like to leave Mirandolina like this.

CAVALIERE: No more do I. The very thought of leaving here fills me with a reluctance I never felt before. All the more reason to go. The sooner the better. Women! I shall always have a bad name for them. Even when they mean well, they only mean trouble.

FABRIZIO: [Enters] Is it true, Signore, you want your bill?

CAVALIERE: Yes. Have you got it?

FABRIZIO: The mistress is making it out now.

CAVALIERE: She makes out the bills herself?

FABRIZIO: Who else, signore? She's always done it, even when her father was still alive.

CAVALIERE: (What a remarkable woman she is!)

FABRIZIO: Do you have to leave so soon?

CAVALIERE: Yes... business.

FABRIZIO: You won't be forgetting the waiter, then, signor?

CAVALIERE: Just bring the bill and I shall know quite well what to do.

FABRIZIO: You want it here?

CAVALIERE: Yes, here. I shan't be leaving for the moment.

FABRIZIO: Very wise, signore. The Marchese is on the watch for you. He's a bore and a nuisance. Thinks he going to be the mistress's lover. Much good that'll do him. Mirandolina's going to marry me.

CAVALIERE: [*Angrily*] The bill!

FABRIZIO: At once. [*Goes*]

CAVALIERE: Are the whole lot of them in love with her? No wonder, I suppose, if I nearly began to think possibly of the idea of falling for her myself. But I shall get away - conquer this mysterious force of nature... Who's coming? Mirandolina! With a ledger in her hand. What does she want? She's bringing me the bill. What should I do? Withstand the final onslaught? In two hours from now, I leave.

MIRANDOLINA: [*Sadly*] Signore...

CAVALIERE: What is it, Mirandolina?

MIRANDOLINA: [*Staying by the door*] Forgive me.

CAVALIERE: Come in.

MIRANDOLINA: You asked for your bill; I have made it out.

CAVALIERE: Give it to me.

MIRANDOLINA: [*Wiping her eyes on her apron*] Here.

CAVALIERE: What is the matter? Are you crying?

MIRANDOLINA: It's nothing, signore, some smoke must have got in my eyes.

CAVALIERE: Smoke... in your eyes? Well, what does it come to then? [*Reading the bill*] Twenty florins? Four days, and such service - only twenty florins?

MIRANDOLINA: That is your bill.

CAVALIERE: But those two special dishes you gave me today, are they not on the bill?

MIRANDOLINA: Forgive me. What I give people I do not charge for.

CAVALIERE: They were presents?

MIRANDOLINA: Please forgive the liberty. And accept them as an act... [*Covers her face, as if in tears*]

CAVALIERE: But what is the matter?

MIRANDOLINA: I don't know if it's the smoke, or something wrong with my eyes.

CAVALIERE: I hope not through cooking those delicious things for me.

MIRANDOLINA: Oh, if it were that, I'd suffer ... gladly...

CAVALIERE: (I must get away!) Look. Here are two crowns. Enjoy yourself for my sake - to remember - me sometimes, and be sorry for me... [*He loses himself, confounded. MIRANDOLINA falls in a faint*] Mirandolina! Oh, my God, she's fainted! Can she be in love with me? But as quickly as that? And why not, indeed? If I can fall in love with her? Mirandolina dearest... What am I doing, endearments to a woman? But if she's fainted - and because of me? Oh, beautiful! I've nothing to help bring her round. Women's things, salts, scents, feathers? Ehi, is anybody there?! Where are they all? I'll go myself! Oh, my poor, dear, girl! God bless you!

[*He goes*]

MIRANDOLINA: [*Alone*] There! I've done it! Women have so many weapons to bring men down. But when the foe is stubborn, one must bring up the reserves, and the biggest of the big guns is a well-timed faint. Here he comes. To your post! [*Collapses again*]

CAVALIERE: [*Returning with a glass of water*] Here I am, here I am. She's still unconscious. There's no doubt of it - she loves me. [*Sprinkles water on her, she stirs*] Come on, come on. *Cara, carissima*, I'm here. I shan't leave you now - ever.

STEFANO: [*Entering*] Here are your sword and hat.

CAVALIERE: Get out !

STEFANO: The luggage...

CAVALIERE: Get out, damn your eyes!

STEFANO: Oh!... Mirandolina...

CAVALIERE: [*Furious*] Get out or I'll crack  your skull for you! [*STEFANO, threatened with the glass by the CAVALIERE, goes*] she still hasn't come round. Her forehead is all wet. Come on, Mirandolina, Mirandolina dearest, be brave, open  your eyes. Speak to me!

MARCHESE: [*Entering with the CONTE*] Cavaliere!

CONTE: Oh, I say!

CAVALIERE: (Damn the pair of them!)

MARCHESE: Mirandolina!

MIRANDOLINA: Oh, heavens, heavens!

MARCHESE: There! Brought her round in no time.

CONTE: I congratulate you, Cavaliere.

MARCHESE: Yes, very well done - for a man who can't bear women.

CAVALIERE: What the devil are you suggesting?

CONTE: Succumbed as well?

CAVALIERE: Go to the devil - the whole pack of you! [*He smashes the glass on the floor in front of the MARCHESE and the CONTE, and flings out in a fury*]

CONTE: Fellow's gone mad!

MARCHESE: That was an insult! I demand satisfaction! [*They run out*]

MIRANDOLINA: [*Alone*] *Vittoria*! *Vittoria*! The day is carried! The barricades are breached and down, the ramparts assaulted! His heart kindles, catches, flares, flames, blazes, scorches, sputters and burns to ashes. All that remains to assure my triumph is to hold my victory parade in public to the scorn of presumptuous men and the honour of my sex.

"If love can once Presumption's outworks win,
It swiftly conquers all that lies within.
But I have weapons primed to main and kill;
There's no deep valley but near some great hill."

□

# ACT THREE

## SCENE 1

A room with laundry waiting to be ironed.

MIRANDOLINA: Well, now the time for amusing myself is over, and I have a business to run. I must iron this laundry before it dries out completely. Ehi, Fabrizio!

FABRIZIO: [*Appearing*] Signora.

MIRANDOLINA: Do me a favour and fetch me a hot iron.

FABRIZIO: [*Glumly, making to go*] Signora.

MIRANDOLINA: I'm sorry if it's a nuisance.

FABRIZIO: Not at all, signora. I eat your bread, so I am obliged to do what I'm told. [*Making to go again*]

MIRANDOLINA: Just a minute; listen to me: you are not *obliged* to do anything of the sort; but I know you do things willingly for me, and as for me ... well, that's enough of that for the moment.

FABRIZIO: I'd work my fingers to the elbow for you. But I see it's all thrown away.

MIRANDOLINA: What do you mean - thrown away? Do you think I'm ungrateful?

FABRIZIO: You don't bother to notice poor men. You're too interested in the aristocracy.

MIRANDOLINA: You're mad! If I were to tell you everything... Oh, run along and fetch me that iron.

FABRIZIO: But the things I've seen with my own eyes...

MIRANDOLINA: Run along and stop moping. Bring me the iron.

FABRIZIO: [*Going*] I'm going, I'm going, I'll do what I'm told, but not for much longer.

MIRANDOLINA: [*Sotto voce, but meaning to be heard*] These men, the nicer you are to them, the worse it is.

FABRIZIO: [*Turning back, gently*] What did you say?

MIRANDOLINA: Are you going for that iron or not?

FABRIZIO: Yes, yes. (I don't know what's going on)

MIRANDOLINA: (Poor boy! He can't help doing what I ask)

FABRIZIO: (One minute she's leading me on)

MIRANDOLINA: (But making men do what I want is amusing)

FABRIZIO: (The next she's sending me packing. I don't understand)
[*Goes*]

MIRANDOLINA: This Cavaliere now, the great foe of Womankind, I could make him jump through a few hoops if I chose.

STEFANO: [*Entering*] Signora Mirandolina.

MIRANDOLINA: Yes, friend, what is it?

STEFANO: My master sends his compliments and has sent to see how you are.

MIRANDOLINA: Tell him I am very well.

STEFANO: [*Giving her a little gold bottle*] He says you should drink a little of this, it's spirits of Melissa, it will do you good.

MIRANDOLINA: Is that bottle gold?

STEFANO: Yes, signora, I can vouch for that.

MIRANDOLINA: Why didn't he give me some of this before, when I had that terrible fainting-fit?

STEFANO: He didn't have this bottle then.

MIRANDOLINA: And how does he come to have it now?

STEFANO: Listen. In confidence. He sent me to find a goldsmith, he bought it, and paid twelve guineas for it; then he sent me to the chemist to buy the Melissa. What are you laughing at?

MIRANDOLINA: Sending me the cure when I've got over the trouble.

STEFANO: It'll do for another time.

MIRANDOLINA: Go on, I'll drink a little for safety's sake. [*Drinks*] There you are, then. Thank him for me. [*Gives the bottle back*]

STEFANO: Oh, the bottle is for you.

MIRANDOLINA: What do you mean, me?

STEFANO: The master bought it specially .

MIRANDOLINA: Specially for me?

STEFANO: Yes, you: but don't say I said.

MIRANDOLINA: Take him back his bottle, and say I thank him.

STEFANO: Oh, I...

MIRANDOLINA: I'm telling you to take it back, I don't want it.

STEFANO: You mean you want to insult him?

MIRANDOLINA: Less chatter. Do as you're told. Take it back.

STEFANO: Well, I don't know! I'll take it back then. (What a woman! Turning down twelve guineas! I've never found another like her, and I'll have a hard job to do so!) [*Goes out*]

MIRANDOLINA: [*Alone*] He is toasted, roasted, basted, cooked and hooked! But what I did was not just self-interest. I just want him to admit that women can have power over men, without saying they have to be venal, self-seeking harpies.

FABRIZIO: [*Entering*] The iron.

MIRANDOLINA: Is it good and hot?

FABRIZIO: Yes, signora - like me.

MIRANDOLINA: What's the matter now?

FABRIZIO: That Cavaliere is sending you messages, and presents. His servant just told me.

MIRANDOLINA: Yes, Signore, he has. He sent me a little gold bottle, and I sent it right back.

FABRIZIO: You sent it back?

MIRANDOLINA: Ask the servant.

FABRIZIO: But why did you send it back?

MIRANDOLINA: Because... Fabrizio... I'm not going to... let's change the subject.

FABRIZIO: Mirandolina, please, have pity on me!

MIRANDOLINA: Go away, let me do my ironing.

FABRIZIO: I'm not stopping you from...

MIRANDOLINA: Go and get another iron ready, and bring it when it's hot.

FABRIZIO: All right, I'm going. Believe me, if I say...

MIRANDOLINA: Say another word and you'll drive me mad.

FABRIZIO: Not another word. (I'm the one who'll be driven mad. But I love her) [*Goes*]

MIRANDOLINA: [*Getting on with the ironing*] That all worked out quite well. By refusing the Cavaliere's bottle, I pleased Fabrizio at any rate. That is what people mean when they talk about knowing how to manage one's life, behave well and turn everything to good use, with good grace, good manners and good sense.

CAVALIERE: [*Entering*] (There she is. I didn't want to see her: the devil made me come)

MIRANDOLINA: [*Catching him out of the corner of her eye*] (Here he is! here he is!)

CAVALIERE: Mirandolina?

MIRANDOLINA: [*Ironing*] Oh, signor Cavaliere! Your servant.

CAVALIERE: How are you?

MIRANDOLINA: [*Ironing, not looking at him*] Very well, thank you.

CAVALIERE: You have made me very unhappy.

MIRANDOLINA: [*A glance at him*] How would that be, Signore?

CAVALIERE: Refusing that little bottle I sent.

MIRANDOLINA: What did you want me to do with it?

CAVALIERE: Use it, when you needed it.

MIRANDOLINA: For Heaven's sake, I'm not subject to fainting-fits. Today was something that's never happened to me before.

CAVALIERE: Mirandolina... dearest... I would not like to think I had been the cause of such a... unfortunate turn of events.

MIRANDOLINA: Oh, yes, I am afraid you were.

CAVALIERE: [With passion] Really? Was I?

MIRANDOLINA: [Ironing furiously] You made me drink that wretched Frascati. And it made me ill.

CAVALIERE: [Mortified] Do you mean that? Is it possible?

MIRANDOLINA: Very much so. I shan't be visiting your room again.

CAVALIERE: Ah, I understand. You don't wish to be seen dining with me any more. So that's all! You had me quite mystified! Now I understand. But come here now, my dearest, and let that make you happy.

MIRANDOLINA: This iron is hardly warm. Ehi! Fabrizio! If the other iron is hot, bring it here.

CAVALIERE: Be kind to me - accept the bottle..

MIRANDOLINA: Really, Signor Cavaliere, I cannot accept presents.

CAVALIERE: You do from the Conte.

MIRANDOLINA: I had to - so as not to offend him.

CAVALIERE: But you're happy enough to offend me?

MIRANDOLINA: What does it matter to you if a woman offends you? You can't stand the sight of them.

CAVALIERE: Ah, Mirandolina, I cannot say that any more.

MIRANDOLINA: Signor Cavaliere - when did the moon change?

CAVALIERE: It's nothing to do with the moon. The miracle has been worked by your beauty and your charm. Why do you laugh?

MIRANDOLINA: Should I not? You make fun of me, and don't want me to laugh?

CAVALIERE: You think I'm making fun of you? Here, take the bottle.

MIRANDOLINA: [Ironing] Thank you - no.

CAVALIERE: Take it or I shall lose my temper.

MIRANDOLINA: Fabrizio! The iron!

CAVALIERE: [Angrily] Will you or will you not take it?

MIRANDOLINA: Temper, temper. [she takes the bottle and throws it contemptuously into the laundry basket]

CAVALIERE: How dare you throw it away like that?

MIRANDOLINA: Fabrizio!!

FABRIZIO: [*Entering with the iron*] Here I am. [*With a jealous glance at the* CAVALIERE]

MIRANDOLINA: Nice and hot, is it?

FABRIZIO: Yes, signora.

MIRANDOLINA: [*With solicitude*] What is the matter? You look put out.

FABRIZIO: Nothing, signora, nothing.

MIRANDOLINA: Aren't you feeling well?

FABRIZIO: Give me the other iron, if you want it put on the stove.

MIRANDOLINA: No, really, I'm afraid you're not well.

CAVALIERE: Just give him the iron and let him get out.

MIRANDOLINA: [*To the* CAVALIERE] I'm concerned about him, you understand? He's a very loyal servant.

CAVALIERE: [*In despair*] (I'm at my wit's end)

MIRANDOLINA: Here, my dear, heat it up.

FABRIZIO: [*Languishing*] Ah, signora...

MIRANDOLINA: [*Chasing him out*] Out, out, out.

FABRIZIO: [*Going*] (What sort of a life is this? I'm at my wit's end)

CAVALIERE: Very kind to your waiter, are you not, signorina?

MIRANDOLINA: And what is that supposed to mean?

CAVALIERE: It's obvious you're in love with him.

MIRANDOLINA: In love with a waiter? What a nice compliment, signore: I have better taste than that. When I decide to fall in love, I shall not be throwing myself away so cheaply.

CAVALIERE: You are worthy of the love of a king!

MIRANDOLINA: The king of spades or the king of clubs?

CAVALIERE: I'm not joking, Mirandolina. Be serious.

MIRANDOLINA: Talk then. I'm listening.

CAVALIERE: Can't you leave those damn sheets alone for five seconds?

MIRANDOLINA: Oh, excuse me! I have to have all these ready for tomorrow.

CAVALIERE: Is your laundry more important to you than me?

MIRANDOLINA: Yes.

CAVALIERE: You mean that?

MIRANDOLINA: Of course. This laundry is my bread and butter. You are not.

CAVALIERE: Mirandolina, I can give you jam.

MIRANDOLINA: A man who can't bear the sight of women?

CAVALIERE: Don't torment me any more. You've had revenge enough. I respect you, I respect women like you - if there are any others. I respect you, I love you, and I ask you for mercy.

MIRANDOLINA: Very well, signore, that is what we'll tell them. [*she drops a cuff, which the CAVALIERE picks up and gives her*]

CAVALIERE: Signorina, you must believe me...

MIRANDOLINA: Please don't bother.

CAVALIERE: You deserve to be waited on. Why do you laugh?

MIRANDOLINA: You're making fun of me again.

CAVALIERE: Mirandolina, I can't go on like this.

MIRANDOLINA: Are you ill?

CAVALIERE: No! Yes, I feel faint.

MIRANDOLINA: [*Throwing the bottle to him casually*] Why don't you try your little bottle, then?

CAVALIERE: Don't treat me so cruelly. Believe me, I love you, I swear it. Ouch! [*He tries to take her hand, and puts his on the hot iron*]

MIRANDOLINA: I'm sorry. I didn't do that on purpose.

CAVALIERE: Never mind! It's nothing. Nothing to the hurt you've already given me.

MIRANDOLINA: Where, signore?

CAVALIERE: My heart.

MIRANDOLINA: [*Laughing*] Fabrizio!

CAVALIERE: For Heaven's sake, don't call for him.

MIRANDOLINA: But I need the other iron.

CAVALIERE: Wait... (but no...) I shall call my servant.

MIRANDOLINA: Ehi, Fabrizio!

CAVALIERE: I swear to God, if that fellow comes in here, I'll crack his skull!

MIRANDOLINA: Oh, are my own servants not allowed to work for me now?

CAVALIERE: Then call someone else. I can't stand the sight of him.

MIRANDOLINA: [*Keeping him at a distance with the iron*] It seems to me you're getting a touch close, Signor Cavaliere.

CAVALIERE: Have pity! I don't know what I'm doing.

MIRANDOLINA: I shall go to the kitchen; then you'll be all right.

CAVALIERE: No, my love, don't go.

MIRANDOLINA: [*Pacing*] (This is all very odd)

CAVALIERE: Have mercy on me!

MIRANDOLINA: Can I not call whom I wish?

CAVALIERE: [*Following her*] Very well. I admit. I'm jealous of him.

MIRANDOLINA: (Following me round like a little dog)

CAVALIERE: This is the first time I have discovered what love is.

MIRANDOLINA: [*Pacing*] No one has ever ordered me about before.

CAVALIERE: I never meant to order you - I'm begging you.

MIRANDOLINA: [*Turning angrily*] What is it you want of me?

CAVALIERE: Love, compassion, pity.

MIRANDOLINA: A man who couldn't look at a woman this morning, is asking for love and pity from one this afternoon? I don't understand you, I don't take you seriously, I don't believe you! (Rant away, till you burst, and learn what it is to despise women !) [*she goes out*]

CAVALIERE: [*Alone*] Damn the moment I first set eyes on that woman! I've fallen into the trap. There is no cure.

MARCHESE: [*Enters*] Cavaliere, you have insulted me.

CAVALIERE: I'm sorry, it was an accident.

MARCHESE: I am amazed at you.

CAVALIERE: The glass didn't hit you, after all.

MARCHESE: A drop of water has stained my waistcoat.

CAVALIERE: I repeat, I'm sorry.

MARCHESE: This is a dratted impertinence.

CAVALIERE: I did not do it on purpose. For the third time - I'm sorry.

MARCHESE: I demand satisfaction.

CAVALIERE: If you won't accept my apology, if you insist on satisfaction - I am here. I'm not going to be imposed on by you.

MARCHESE: [*Changing his tone*] I'm worried the stain may not come out: that is what is annoying me.

CAVALIERE: When a gentleman has offered an apology, what more can he do?

MARCHESE: If you didn't do it to spite me, we'll say no more about it.

CAVALIERE: I repeat, I am ready to give you all the satisfaction you could want.

MARCHESE: No, no, let's change the subject.

CAVALIERE: Common snob!

MARCHESE: I beg your pardon. I have recovered my composure, and now you are losing yours.

CAVALIERE: You've caught me at a bad moment.

MARCHESE: I'm sorry for you, I know what you are suffering. And what from.

CAVALIERE: Do I stick my nose into your business?

MARCHESE: Signor Woman-hater - taken the infection eh?

CAVALIERE: I? What?

MARCHESE: Yes, you're in love.

CAVALIERE: Go to Hell!

MARCHESE: What is the good of hiding it?

CAVALIERE: Just leave me alone, or I swear to Heaven, you'll regret it. [*He goes*]

MARCHESE: [*Alone*] In love, and ashamed of it, and doesn't want anyone to know. Or maybe he doesn't want it known, because he's afraid of me, doesn't want to declare himself my rival. This stain is really very annoying - if only I knew how to get it out! These women usually have things like fuller's earth for removing stains. [*He looks on the ironing table and in the basket*] What a pretty little bottle! Gold or Pinchbeck? It'll be Pinchbeck; if it was gold it would hardly be left lying round here; if it had *eau de cologne* in it that might take the stain out. [*Opens it, sniffs and identifies it*] Melissa spirits. Better still. I'll try it.

DEJANIRA: [*Entering*] Signor Marchese, you are too much alone. Are we never to be graced with your company?

MARCHESE: Oh, signora Contessa, I was this minute coming - to you.

DEJANIRA: What were you doing?

MARCHESE: I will tell you. I am a demon for cleanliness. I was removing this spot.

DEJANIRA: With what, Marchese?

MARCHESE: Melissa spirits.

DEJANIRA: Oh, but excuse me, that is no good whatever, it just makes the stain spread.

MARCHESE: Then what can I do?

DEJANIRA: I have a secret remedy for spots.

MARCHESE: It would give me infinite pleasure to hear you impart it.

DEJANIRA: Willingly. For a sovereign I will engage to lift that spot, so no one would ever know there had been one there. Ever.

MARCHESE: You want a sovereign?

DEJANIRA: Yes, Signore, is that such a great outlay?

MARCHESE: Had we not better try the spirits first?

DEJANIRA: [*Making to take the bottle*] Excuse me, are they all right?

MARCHESE: Excellent: smell.

DEJANIRA: What a pretty bottle! Gold?

MARCHESE: Most certainly it is gold. (She can't tell gold from Pinchbeck)

DEJANIRA: Is it yours, signor?

MARCHESE: Most certainly, and yours, if you wish.

DEJANIRA: [*Pocketing it*] Sir, you vanquish me with your civility.

MARCHESE: Ah, I know you're joking.

DEJANIRA: What? Was that not why you exposed it to me?

MARCHESE: A thing far below your worth. A mere kickshaw. Between you and me, it's not gold. It's Pinchbeck.

DEJANIRA: All the better. I shall esteem it the more. Anything from your hand is as precious as it is rare.

MARCHESE: Enough. I don't know what to say. Keep it. If you want it. (Damnation. Now I shall have to pay Mirandolina for it. What is it worth? A few shillings? No more, surely)

DEJANIRA: The Signor Marchese is a man of largesse.

MARCHESE: I am ashamed to present you with such bagatelles. I wish it really were gold.

DEJANIRA: It looks like gold. Anybody would be deceived.

MARCHESE: Anybody unacquainted with gold, true. But I knew at once.

DEJANIRA: It weighs like gold, too.

MARCHESE: But it isn't.

DEJANIRA: I must show it to my friend.

MARCHESE: Listen, signora Contessa, don't let Mirandolina see it, if you please. She is something of a tattle. I don't know if you take my meaning.

DEJANIRA: Perfectly, Marchese. I shall show it only to Ortensia.

MARCHESE: To the Baronessa?

DEJANIRA: The what? Oh, yes, the Baronessa. Hahaha. [*she goes out*]

MARCHESE: [*Alone*] I expect they will have a fine laugh at having wheedled it out of me. Just as well it wasn't real gold. Oh, well, if it comes to the worst, I can always put the matter right. If Mirandolina must have her little bottle, I can pay for it - when I can. [*STEFANO enters and rummages under the table*] What are you looking for, my man?

STEFANO: A little bottle of spirits. The Signora Mirandolina wants it. She says she left it here, but I can't find it.

MARCHESE: A little Pinchbeck bottle?

STEFANO: Oh, no, signore, it was real gold.

MARCHESE: Real - gold?

STEFANO: [*Hunting for it*] Yes, of course. I saw it bought and paid for, twelve guineas.

MARCHESE: (Oh, heavens!) But why was a gold bottle just left lying around?

STEFANO: she forgot it. But I can't find it.

MARCHESE: It can't have been gold.

STEFANO: It was, I tell you. Perhaps *Eccellenza* has seen it?

MARCHESE: I?... I've seen nothing.

STEFANO: Well, I'll just have to tell her I can't find it. Her loss. She should have put it in her pocket. [*He goes out*]

MARCHESE: [*Alone*] Ah, Forlipopoli, you are undone. Here you have given away a gold bottle worth twenty guineas: you took it for Pinchbeck, and the Contessa just took it. If I recover the bottle I shall look a fool in the Contessa's eyes: if Mirandolina discovers it, I shall look a thief in hers. How is a man of standing to behave in a situation of such importance and delicacy? I am a man of honour. I must pay her. But I have no money. All is lost - save honour, and what good is that to him that died on Wednesday? "Can Honour's voice invoke the silent dust, Or flattery soothe the dull, cold ear of Death?" Oh, Marchese, Marchese of most ill fortune, is truth nowhere to be found, but at the bottom of a well?

CONTE: [*Entering*] Well, Marchese, what do you say of the great news?

MARCHESE: What news?

CONTE: The Grand Misogynist, the Cavaliere - is in love - with Mirandolina.

MARCHESE: Yes... I've been wondering about that. Even he can recognise the worth of that woman; he can see that I would never show an interest in one who did not deserve it; and he can suffer and die for his impertinence.

CONTE: But what if Mirandolina should return his feelings?

MARCHESE: Out of the question. She would not do me such a wrong. She knows who I am. She knows what I have done for her.

CONTE: I've done a sight more for her than you have. But it was a waste of effort. Mirandolina is encouraging the Cavaliere di Ripafratta, she has paid him attentions she has never paid you - or me; and it's clear that with women, the more you do the less you get. They laugh at those who adore them, and run after those who despise them.

MARCHESE: If that were true... but it can't be.

CONTE: Why not?

MARCHESE: You can't be comparing the Cavaliere with me, can you?

CONTE: Didn't you see her yourself, sitting at his table? Has she ever committed an act of such intimacy with us? He gets special linen. His meals are served first. Special dishes are prepared for him with her own hands. The servants see it all, and they talk. Fabrizio is eaten up with jealousy. And that fainting-fit, genuine or feigned, whichever, wasn't that a declaration of love?

MARCHESE: What! She made him a ragout, and I had nothing but plain beef and rice soup? Yes, indeed! That is an insult to my rank, my position.

CONTE: What about me, spending all that on her?

MARCHESE: And I, who showered her with gifts? I even gave her some of my priceless Cyprus wine. The Cavaliere won't have done the smallest part of what we've done for her.

CONTE: Oh, don't think he hasn't given her things.

MARCHESE: Oh, yes? What has he given her?

CONTE: A little gold bottle of Melissa.

MARCHESE: (Ahi!) How did you know that?

CONTE: His servant told me.

MARCHESE: (Worse and worse. This will mean trouble with the Cavaliere as well)

CONTE: I see now she has no idea of the meaning of gratitude; I shall let her drop completely. I wish to leave this rubbishy inn this minute.

MARCHESE: Yes, you're right, you should leave.

CONTE: And you who are a nobleman of such standing should leave with me.

MARCHESE: But... where would one go?

CONTE: We shall go to the house of one of my countrymen. We'll have nothing to pay there.

MARCHESE: Say no more. I cannot refuse such an offer from a good friend.

CONTE: Let us go, then, and revenge ourselves on this ungrateful woman.

MARCHESE: Yes, let us go. (But what about that bottle? A man of my standing... I cannot be thought a thief)

CONTE: No second thoughts, Marchese, let us get away from here. Back me up in this matter, and I shall be yours to command, insofar as I can be.

MARCHESE: I say... in strictest confidence... wouldn't want anyone to know... my factor is sometimes somewhat remiss in remitting my remittances...

CONTE: You mean you can't pay your bill here?

MARCHESE: That's it - twelve guineas.

CONTE: Twelve guineas! You can't have paid her for months!

MARCHESE: Well, that is how it is - I owe her twelve guineas. I can't leave here without paying. If you could oblige me...

CONTE: [*Taking out his purse*] Of course. Here.

MARCHESE: Wait! Now I come to think - it's thirteen. (I must give the Cavaliere back his guinea)

CONTE: Twelve, thirteen, what's the odds? There.

MARCHESE: I will pay you back just as soon as ever I can.

CONTE: Whenever you please. Money is no object - I'd give a thousand crowns to pay that woman back.

MARCHESE: Yes, she really is ungrateful. I've spent a fortune on her, and to be treated like this!

CONTE: I'm going to ruin this inn! I've made those actresses leave too.

MARCHESE: What actresses?

CONTE: Those two spurious countesses who were staying here.

MARCHESE: You mean they weren't - ladies?

CONTE: Not in a million years! Their company arrived, and the myth was exploded.

MARCHESE: (My bottle!) Where have they gone?

CONTE: A house next door to the theatre.

MARCHESE: [*Leaving precipitately*] (I must go at once and get the bottle back)

CONTE: That can be my revenge on *him*. Now for the Cavaliere, putting on his act to deceive me. I've another way to settle *his* hash. [*Leaves*]

# SCENE 2

A room with three doors

MIRANDOLINA: [*Alone*] This is terrible. What have I got myself into? If the Cavaliere comes here, I am done for. The devil must have got into him; and I don't want the devil tempting him to come here. Lock the door. [*She locks the door she came in by*] I'm beginning to wish I hadn't started all this. True, it amused me no end making him run after me, with all his stuffiness and woman-hating; but now he's like a satyr, pursued by furies, and I can see the danger to my reputation, my life even. I must make a decision, and an important one. I'm on my own, I've no one of any consequence to defend me. Only Fabrizio. There's always Fabrizio. I'll promise to marry him... but I've cried "Wolf!" on that so often, he won't believe me any more. It might be better if I really did marry him. A marriage like that - I'd be able to safeguard my own interests and my reputation, and still not lose my freedom. [*A violent knocking at the door*] What a racket! Who is it?

CAVALIERE: [*Off*] Mirandolina!

MIRANDOLINA: (Ah! My friend!)

CAVALIERE: Mirandolina, let me in!

MIRANDOLINA: (I'm not such a fool) What is it you want, Cavaliere?

CAVALIERE: Open the door.

MIRANDOLINA: Please go back to your room, and wait for me there.

CAVALIERE: Why won't you open the door?

MIRANDOLINA: Some guests have just arrived. Please, do what I ask, and I will be with you in a minute.

CAVALIERE: All right. But if you don't - woe betide you!

MIRANDOLINA: And woe betide me if I do go. Things are going from bad to worse. I must do something. Has he gone? [*Looking through the keyhole*] Yes, he has. He's waiting in his room, but I'm not going there. [*Going to another door*] Ehi! Fabrizio! What will I do if Fabrizio decides to have his revenge, and won't...? Oh, no danger of that. I have my ways and means, that would melt him if he were made of rock. [*Calling at another door*] Fabrizio!

FABRIZIO: Did you call?

MIRANDOLINA: Come here - I've something to tell you... in confidence.

FABRIZIO: Here I am.

MIRANDOLINA: The Cavaliere has discovered he is in love with me.

FABRIZIO: Yes, I'd noticed.

MIRANDOLINA: You had? You'd noticed? But I had really no idea myself.

FABRIZIO: You poor child! You didn't notice? While you were doing the ironing, you didn't notice him mincing around you, you didn't notice how jealous he was of me?

MIRANDOLINA: If you act without malice yourself, it's hard to spot in others. But he has been saying things which, really Fabrizio, which made me blush!

FABRIZIO: It's because you're a young woman on her own, no father, no mother, no one. It wouldn't happen if you were married.

MIRANDOLINA: Yes, I know you're right: I have been thinking about marriage.

FABRIZIO: Remember what your father said.

MIRANDOLINA: I am remembering. [*CAVALIERE knocks at the door*] Someone's knocking.

FABRIZIO: Who is it?

CAVALIERE: Open this door!

MIRANDOLINA: The Cavaliere!

FABRIZIO: [*At the door*] What do you want?

MIRANDOLINA: Wait till I've gone.

FABRIZIO: [*To MIRANDOLINA*] What are you frightened of?

MIRANDOLINA: [*Going*] Dear Fabrizio ... I don't know ... I'm afraid of my own feelings.

FABRIZIO: Don't be afraid, I'll see you're all right.

CAVALIERE: Open this door, or I swear to Heaven...

FABRIZIO: What is it you want, signore? What's all the shouting? This is no way to behave in a respectable hotel.

CAVALIERE: [*Trying to force the door*] Open this damned door!

FABRIZIO: For Heaven's sake, he'll have the door in! Ehi, who's there? Is nobody there?

CONTE and MARCHESE: [*Entering by another door, speaking together*] What is the matter? What's all this noise?

FABRIZIO: [*Quietly to them*] Signori, please - it's the Cavaliere, he's trying to force the door.

CAVALIERE: Will you open this door, or do I have to break it down?

MARCHESE: He's gone mad! Let's go.

CONTE: [*To FABRIZIO*] Open it. I've a few words to say to him.

FABRIZIO: All right, but please...

CONTE: That's all right. We are here.

MARCHESE: (The first sign of trouble and I'm off)

CAVALIERE: [*Coming in as FABRIZIO opens the door*] Well, then, where is she?

FABRIZIO: Who are you looking for, signore?

CAVALIERE: Where is Mirandolina?

FABRIZIO: I don't know.

MARCHESE: (It's all right. He wants Mirandolina)

CAVALIERE: Little wretch! Wait till I get hold of her!

CONTE: What is the matter with you?

MARCHESE: Cavaliere, we are your friends.

CAVALIERE: (The devil! I don't want my weakness shown up for all the money in the world)

FABRIZIO: What was it you wanted of the mistress, signora?

CAVALIERE: None of your business. When I give an order, I expect it to be carried out. That is what I pay good money for, or I swear to Heaven, she will have me to deal with.

FABRIZIO: *Illustrissimo*, you pay good money to be served honestly and legitimately: but that does not, if you will excuse me, entitle you to expect an honest woman to...

CAVALIERE: What are you talking about? What do you know about it? You have nothing to do with it. I know the orders gave her.

FABRIZIO: You asked her to come to your room.

CAVALIERE: Get out, you damned fellow, or I'll break your neck!

FABRIZIO: Would you now? I'm amazed at you ...

MARCHESE: Oh, hush.

CONTE: Go away!

CAVALIERE: Get out!

FABRIZIO: But, gentlemen, I tell you, he...

CONTE and MARCHESE: [*Together*] Out!

FABRIZIO: [*Chased away by them*] (Dear Heavens, only too glad to get out of here!)

CAVALIERE: (Wretched little creature! Making me kick my heels in my room!)

MARCHESE: [*Aside to the CONTE*] What the devil's the matter with him?

CONTE: Can't you see? He's in love with Mirandolina.

CAVALIERE: (Has she got that Fabrizio on a string as well? Is she talking to him about marriage?)

CONTE: (Time for my revenge) Signor Cavaliere, it is hardly the thing to laugh at the weaknesses of others, with a heart as fragile as your own.

CAVALIERE: Just what do you mean by that?

CONTE: I am quite aware of the cause of your insanity.

CAVALIERE: [*Angrily, to the MARCHESE*] Have you any idea what he is talking about?

MARCHESE: Friend, I know - nothing.

CONTE: I'm talking about you. Claiming you couldn't stand the sight of women, then you try and ravish the heart of Mirandolina, when she was already my conquest.

CAVALIERE: [*To the MARCHESE, as before*] Is he talking about me?

MARCHESE: I say - nothing.

CONTE: Have the goodness to answer me to my face. Are you not ashamed of having proceeded in this fashion?

CAVALIERE: The only thing I'm ashamed of is listening to you any longer without telling you you're a liar!

CONTE: I - am a liar?

MARCHESE: (Things are getting worse!)

CAVALIERE: What grounds have you for saying such things? [*Angrily to the MARCHESE*] (The Conte doesn't know what he's talking about)

MARCHESE: I have no wish to be mixed up in this.

CONTE: You're the one who's the liar!

MARCHESE: [*Making to go*] I'm off.

CAVALIERE: [*Holding him back*] You are not.

CONTE: And I demand satisfaction.

CAVALIERE: You shall have it... [*To the MARCHESE*] Give me your sword.

MARCHESE: Come, come, calm down, the pair of you. Conte, *caro*, what can you care whether the Cavaliere is in love with Mirandolina?

CAVALIERE: In love with her? It's not true, and anyone who says it is a liar!

MARCHESE: Liar? Me? I'm not the one who's saying it!

CAVALIERE: Then who?

CONTE: I do and maintain it, and I shan't be imposed on by you!

CAVALIERE: [*To MARCHESE*] Give me that sword.

MARCHESE: No.

CAVALIERE: Are you joining the enemy too?

MARCHESE: I am everybody's friend.

CONTE: Your behaviour is not that of a gentleman.

CAVALIERE: By God, you go too far, sir!

[*He pulls at the MARCHESE's sword, which comes out, scabbard and all*]

MARCHESE: [*To the CAVALIERE*] What sort of behaviour is that?

CAVALIERE: You can have satisfaction too if you want.

MARCHESE: No need to lose our temper! (I hate anything like this)

CONTE: [*Standing on guard*] I demand satisfaction!

CAVALIERE: [*Struggling vainly with the scabbard*] You'll get it!

MARCHESE: You don't understand that sword...

CAVALIERE: Confound the damned thing!

MARCHESE: Cavaliere, you'll get nowhere ...

CONTE: My patience is wearing thin!

CAVALIERE: Here! [*Draws the sword, which turns out to be a mere stump*] What the...?

MARCHESE: You've broken my sword!

CAVALIERE: Where's the rest of it? There's nothing in the scabbard.

MARCHESE: Ah, yes, of course, I broke it in my last duel, I'd forgotten.

CAVALIERE: Allow me to fetch my own.

CONTE: By heaven, I'll see you don't wriggle out of this!

CAVALIERE: Wriggle out? I'll fight you with this!

MARCHESE: Have no fear - it is Spanish steel.

CONTE: Not so much boasting, signor - braggart!

CAVALIERE: [*Rushing on the CONTE*] This is enough for you!

CONTE: [*Placing himself in defense*] Have at you, then!

FABRIZIO: [*Entering with MIRANDOLINA*] Gentlemen, put up, put up!

MIRANDOLINA: Stop this at once!

CAVALIERE: [*Seeing her*] (Damnation take her!)

MIRANDOLINA: Swords! In my hotel!

MARCHESE: You see? And all your fault.

MIRANDOLINA: What do you mean my fault?

CONTE: The Cavaliere here - he is in love with you.

CAVALIERE: I? In love? It's not true.

MIRANDOLINA: The Signor Cavaliere in love with me? No, no, Signor
   Conte, you are mistaken. I can assure you, very much mistaken.

CONTE: Oh, come, you are in agreement...

MARCHESE: We know what we've seen...

CAVALIERE: [*Angrily, to the MARCHESE*] Know what? Seen what?

MARCHESE: If it's true, we know... and if it's not, we've not seen.

MIRANDOLINA: The Signor Cavaliere has denied he is in love with me
   - and to my face.. He has humiliated me, slandered me and made me
   see his strength and my weakness. I confess, if I had been able to make
   him fall in love with me, I would have thought I'd achieved the ninth
   wonder of the world. One cannot hope to arouse love in a man who
   despises women, who has such a low opinion of them, who cannot stand
   the sight of them. Signori, I am a simple, straightforward woman - I
   speak when I have to, and I cannot hide the truth. I tried to make the
   Cavaliere fall in love with me, and I failed. That is the truth, isn't it,
   signore? I tried and tried, and could do nothing.

CAVALIERE: (I cannot speak)

CONTE: [*To MIRANDOLINA*] You see! Dumbfounded!

MARCHESE: Hasn't the courage to deny it.

CAVALIERE: [*Angrily to the MARCHESE*] You don't know what you're
   talking about!

MARCHESE: [*Sweetly*] Always picking on me!

MIRANDOLINA: No, the Cavaliere is not in love! He knows his way
   round women. He knows their tricks, he doesn't believe their words,
   he doesn't trust their tears. Even when they faint, he laughs.

CAVALIERE: Are the tears of women false, then... are their fainting-fit just feigned?

MIRANDOLINA: What? Didn't you know that, or are you pretending you didn't?

CAVALIERE: By God in Heaven, falsity like that deserves a knife through the heart.

MIRANDOLINA: Signor Cavaliere, do not become too hot, or these gentlemen will think you really are in love.

CONTE: Yes, he is, he can't hide it.

MARCHESE: You can see it in his eyes.

CAVALIERE: No, I am not.

MIRANDOLINA: No, signori, he is not in love. I tell you, I stand by it, and I am ready to prove it.

CAVALIERE: (I can't go on) Conte, another time you will find me provided with a sword.

[*He throws away the stump of the MARCHESE's sword*]

MARCHESE: Careful! That hilt cost money!

MIRANDOLINA: Wait, Cavaliere, it is a matter of your reputation. These gentlemen believe you to be in love. You must undeceive them.

CAVALIERE: I must do nothing of the kind.

MIRANDOLINA: Yes, signore, you must. It will only take a moment.

CAVALIERE: (What is she driving at now?)

MIRANDOLINA: Signori, the most certain indication of love is jealousy,and where there is no jealousy there is no love. If the Signor Cavaliere loved me, he could not accept I should belong to anyone else, but he will accept it and you shall see ...

CAVALIERE: Who is it?

MIRANDOLINA: The one my father chose for me.

FABRIZIO: [*To MIRANDOLINA*] You... don't mean me?

MIRANDOLINA: Yes, Fabrizio, my dear, in the presence of these gentlemen, I give you my hand in marriage.

CAVALIERE: (Oh, God! With him! I cannot bear it!)

MARCHESE: [*To the CONTE*] (Always knew she had a soft spot for the fellow. I told you)

CONTE: (If she's marrying Fabrizio,she can't be in love with the Cavaliere) Yes, marry him, and I'll promise you three hundred pounds.

MARCHESE: Mirandolina, better an egg today than a chicken tomorrow. Marry him this minute and I'll give you twelve guineas on the spot.

MIRANDOLINA: Thank you, signori. But I do not need a dowry. I am a plain girl, with none of the gifts and graces that would fit me to love people of quality or standing. But Fabrizio loves me, and here, and now, in front of you all, I take him...

CAVALIERE: Damn you, then marry whom you please. I know you have tricked me, I know you are congratulating yourself inside for having humiliated me, and I can see the lengths to which you would like to stretch my forbearance. What your deception deserves is a dagger in the heart, and that heart cut out and shown as a warning to all deceiving, flattering women. But that would be debasing myself further still. I shall get out of your sight, cursing your flattery, your tears, your lies. You have made me understand the terrible power your sex can have over us, and taught me, to my cost, that to defeat you, it is not enough to despise you, one must fly from the very sight of you.

[*He goes out*]

CONTE: And he was saying just now he wasn't in love!

MARCHESE: If he tells one more lie I shall demand satisfaction!

MIRANDOLINA: Hush, gentlemen, hush. He has gone, and as long as he does not come back, and as long as this is the end of it, I shall count myself very lucky. Poor man, I succeeded all too well in making him love me, and I exposed myself to a terrible risk. I don't want to run into another. Fabrizio, *caro*, come here and give me your hand.

FABRIZIO: My hand? Not so fast, signora. You make men fall in love with you for amusement, and then expect me to marry you?

MIRANDOLINA: Oh, come, it was all a game. It was silly of me, I know, but I was only a girl, I had no one to order me about. When I am married, things will be different.

FABRIZIO: How different?

STEFANO: [*Entering*] Signora, I came to say goodbye before we leave.

MIRANDOLINA: You are going then?

STEFANO: Yes. My master has gone to the post to have the horses harnessed. He is waiting for me to bring the luggage. We are going to Livorno.

MIRANDOLINA: I'm sorry, if you haven't quite...

STEFANO: I... I've no time to... thank you for everything, and... goodbye. [*He goes*]

MIRANDOLINA: Thanks be to Heaven, they've gone. I am sorry for what happened; he certainly left with a bad taste in his mouth. I shall never play games like that again.

CONTE: Mirandolina, whether you marry or not, I shall not change my feelings for you.

MARCHESE: You can always count on my protection.

MIRANDOLINA: Signori, now I am getting married, I shall not want protectors, nor passions, nor presents. Up to now, I have amused myself, and behaved badly and run too many risks, and I don't want to do so again. This is my husband...

FABRIZIO: Just a minute...

MIRANDOLINA: What do you mean? What is the matter? Where is the difficulty? Come on, give me your hand.

FABRIZIO: I think we should arrange the contracts first.

MIRANDOLINA: What contracts? The contract is very simple; either you give me your hand, or you can go right back where you came from.

FABRIZIO: Yes, I'll give you my hand... but afterwards...

MIRANDOLINA: Afterwards, caro, yes, I shall be all yours. Have no fear. I shall always love you; you will be my heart, my soul, my only love.

FABRIZIO: [Giving his hand] What more could I ask? Here.

MIRANDOLINA: (Then that's settled!)

CONTE: Mirandolina, you are a great woman; you can lead any man where you want.

MARCHESE: Certainly a most obliging manner. Quite - out of the ordinary.

MIRANDOLINA: If it's true that I can rely on your kindness, there is one last favour I would ask.

CONTE: Just say it.

MARCHESE: Speak out.

FABRIZIO: (Now what?)

MIRANDOLINA: Find yourselves another hotel.

FABRIZIO: (So she really does love me!)

CONTE: I understand. Very praiseworthy of you. I shall leave, but, wherever I go, you will always have my admiration.

MARCHESE: Tell me: did you lose a little gold bottle?

MIRANDOLINA: Why, yes, signore.

MARCHESE: La voilà! I found it. I restore it to you. I too shall leave, to put your mind at ease, but throughout the world, you may rest assured of my protection.

MIRANDOLINA: Signori, I shall remember these kind words of yours with an affection bounded only by decency and good behaviour. Changing my state, I mean also to change my habits.

[*To the audience*]
"And you may profit, too, by what you've watched:
The serpent, Love, cannot be killed - just scotched.
When you shall love, and head with heart contend
Whether the reed shall stand, the oak shall bend,
Take note - than women's weapons none are keener.
Pause ere you act: recall... Mirandolina!

## THE END

# Mirandolina
# The Housekeeper

# CHARACTERS

FABRIZIO, an elderly gentleman of means
GIUSEPPINA , his elder niece
ROSINA, his younger niece
VALENTINA, his housekeeper
DOROTEA, maternal aunt of the two girls
FELICITA, Valentina's sister
FULGENZIO, Giuseppina's lover
IPPOLITO, Rosina's lover
BALDISSERA, Valentina's lover
TOGNINO, servant of Fabrizio
NOTARY

*The action takes place in Fabrizio's house in Milan*

This translation was made for the Citizens' Company, and first presented by them at the Citizens' Theatre, Glasgow, on October 5th, 1990, in a production by Robert David MacDonald designed by Michael Levine with the following cast:

Fabrizio, *Andrew Wilde*
Giuseppina, *Anne Marie Timoney*
Rosina, *Debra Gillett*
Valentina, *Julia Blalock*
Dorotea, *Jill Spurrier*
Felicita, *Angela Chadfield*
Fulgenzio, *Derwent Watson*
Ippolito, *Daniel Illsley*
Baldissera, *Eamonn Walker*
Tognino, *Gavin Mitchell*
A Notary, *Matthew Green*

# ACT ONE

[*BALDISSERA alone. Enter VALENTINA. He is about to greet her rapturously, when...*]

VALENTINA: Keep your voice down!

BALDISSERA: Still asleep?

VALENTINA: Yes. We can talk, but quietly; if anyone hears us, they'll tell him the moment he wakes up. I can usually get him to believe anything I want, but with the family so bitterly against me, I'd sooner spare myself the trouble of doing so.

BALDISSERA: Families always hate their fathers' housekeepers. Go by the proverb: if you're clever, say something, and if you're wise, say nothing. No need to be afraid of the police, if you've the magistrate in your pocket.

VALENTINA: I'm not giving that bunch around Signor Fabrizio any chance to attack me. Now his brother is dead, as a man of means, he maintains his two nieces in his house: he shows them little strictness, and they want to see themselves mistresses here. I may have been first taken on to do the rough work in the kitchen, but I am now in sole command under this roof. To colour appearances, he gives me the title of housekeeper; but in practice the old man is so besotted with me...

BALDISSERA: Not too much so, I hope.

VALENTINA: Might you perhaps be jealous?

BALDISSERA: Frankly, a little.

VALENTINA: Poor baby! I hate that kind of tiresomeness. Jealousy is ridiculous nowadays. The days are gone when such passions kept women in subjection; but at least then men too were a touch more controlled, not so often seen in taverns, or gambling rooms, or leaving their place of business to stroll about the piazza with women on their arms. Wives were the temple of wisdom, because they set their husbands a good example. Now that men all follow their own example, how dare they pretend to be jealous of us? You, you brigand, you're full of vices, plain to see, and yet you make a scene because my master kisses me? Start doing some work, set your mind to something; I'll undertake to behave as you want. I love you, I don't deny, but until I can see you keeping me in style, I have no interest in what you have to say. I know what I need, and I don't trust you to provide it. I am clever enough to find a crust with a family. If you cannot bear the pangs of jealousy, then find a job, and fend for yourself.

BALDISSERA: If I could I would, but there's a difficulty.

VALENTINA: Oh?

BALDISSERA: I don't know how to do anything.

VALENTINA: You could go into service.

BALDISSERA: I have my self-respect.

VALENTINA: Servants have to suffer.

BALDISSERA: Not for me.

VALENTINA: You must do *something* in this world.

BALDISSERA: Why? I've done nothing up to now; am I going to die of hunger with a wife at my side?

VALENTINA: Wretch! You're proposing to live off me, and you're not ashamed to talk about jealousy?

BALDISSERA: Valentina, dearest girl, I am delighted to see you doing well, but as a gentleman I don't much care to inquire how. What is the point of telling me the master loves you? That is no fitting talk for a prospective husband. I know you are preferred, no one says you nay, so do your work, do your duty and hold your tongue! Let us speak of lighter things: I need money.

VALENTINA: But I gave you ten ducats last night.

BALDISSERA: What good is that if I've already spent it?

VALENTINA: What on?

BALDISSERA: Must I account to for every penny I spend? I spent them, *basta*. Things for the house: a bed, two pictures and a mirror, two dozen plates, a kettle and a bucket. And a gadget to get the oven going. (Heaven help me if she finds I lost it gambling!)

VALENTINA: Dearest Baldissera, if you have spent it wisely, I will give you whatever you need. But don't be hurt if I also want to know where my money goes. What am I saying, mine? What's mine is thine.

BALDISSERA: Let me have two zecchini, then.

VALENTINA: What for?

BALDISSERA: I owe them to someone. And don't ask any more questions. I'm not a baby: having to be dependent for every blessed thing is not a price at which I am prepared to buy my fortune.

VALENTINA: Don't go away angry. Here you are, take them.

BALDISSERA: Just for this once.

VALENTINA: [*Holding on to the money*] But what are you going to do with them?

BALDISSERA: There you go again! It's really irritating.

VALENTINA: If I am willing to give you what you want, is it so terrible if I want to know how you spend it?

BALDISSERA: It seems you don't trust me: but I'm not throwing it away.

VALENTINA: I know you've been a good boy. I just don't want you gambling.

BALDISSERA: I don't gamble any more.

VALENTINA: Truly?

BALDISSERA: Promise.

VALENTINA: Someone's coming.

BALDISSERA: The money.

VALENTINA: Here.

BALDISSERA: (The dealer betrayed me last night)

VALENTINA: What did you say?

BALDISSERA: I said I made a deal with a trader last night. (I should have bet it all on the Jack) I shall get it all back.

VALENTINA: Take care they don't cheat you.

BALDISSERA: Who do you mean?

VALENTINA: The traders you owe money to, of course.

BALDISSERA: I know my way around.

FABRIZIO: [*Off*] Valentina!

VALENTINA: There's the old man now! Goodbye: come back soon.

BALDISSERA: Yes, my love, goodbye. [*He goes out*]

VALENTINA: Poor Baldissera! I know he loves me. I know he's an honest boy; handsome, friendly, accomplished...

FABRIZIO: [*Off*] Valentina!!

VALENTINA: So different from that ugly bad-tempered old thing! Shouting at everyone, a beast, a fury, but I keep my head; a bit of scolding and a bit of flattery, and I'll fleece him to such a pitch I can marry Baldissera and be a lady.

FABRIZIO: [*Off, louder*] Valentina!!

VALENTINA: He calls for me sixty times a day.

FABRIZIO: [*Louder, approaching*] Valentina!!!

VALENTINA: Lose your breath if you like - what an animal! - and share the fate of other grasshoppers.

FABRIZIO: [*Entering without seeing VALENTINA*] Damnation take the woman! She could break your heart. Where are you, Valenti...[*Seeing her*]

VALENTINA: [*With a caricature of a curtsey*] Signore?

FABRIZIO: I shout and shout, and you don't hear.

VALENTINA: You shout and shout, and you waste your breath.

FABRIZIO: Why don't you answer?

VALENTINA: I was asleep.

FABRIZIO: At this hour?

VALENTINA: At this hour?! It's four hours and more since I've been seeing to the servants in this house. I have had all the rooms swept from floor to ceiling, all the beds shaken and aired, all the copper in the kitchen shined, and with my own hands made the bread and done the laundry. But I wear myself out for nothing. The master screams and shouts all day long. I never saw a worse house. I've said it a hundred times, I want to leave.

FABRIZIO: [*Gently*] You will fly out so suddenly.

VALENTINA: And not for nothing.

FABRIZIO: Was I to know you were asleep?

VALENTINA: Find another woman who will do what I do. If I weren't... but, *basta*, I do my duty and hold my tongue. I'm just sorry I have to do with an ungrateful employer.

FABRIZIO: No, Valentina, my dear, ungrateful I am not. If I said - what I said, I ask your pardon. I have this treacherous nature, I fly out easily, but then I am loving - to all, most of all to you, my dearest. I don't know what I wouldn't do for my Valentina.

VALENTINA: "She could break your heart; damnation take the woman!" I slave and slave, more than you'll ever know, and what thanks do I get?

FABRIZIO: Oh, I could kick myself! [*Beating a fist on his head*]

VALENTINA: (Knock away, there's nobody in)

FABRIZIO: You might sympathise now and then with the foibles of a man who loves you well.

VALENTINA: "Now and then" I could suffer with patience; but shouting all day long! There's no living with it.

FABRIZIO: From now on you'll see - I shall never shout at you again.

VALENTINA: If you were a little gentler, I would go through fire for you. I serve you with love, I am genuinely concerned for the welfare of your house.

FABRIZIO: I know. And one day... *basta*, no more for now. You will never repent the care you take of me. My nieces will be leaving my house soon... one day... eventually... and then... Valentina, you will see what I shall do for you.

VALENTINA: Ah, signor, had I not entered service here, your house would by now be in ruins. Your nieces are a pair of scatterbrains, nothing in their heads but fads or fashions, who would be well able to run through a fortune in a trice - were one to let them. The elder's a proud, affected blue-stocking, too grand to speak to anyone. The other, I admit, is good-natured enough, but under her sister's thumb she gets worse by the moment. And they make love, signore, they are saucy to a point where they bring their lovers into the very house.

FABRIZIO: Lovers?

VALENTINA: Yes.

FABRIZIO: In the house?

VALENTINA: That is so.

FABRIZIO: Giuseppina?

VALENTINA: *Ehi*!

FABRIZIO: Rosina?

VALENTINA: *Mah*!

FABRIZIO: Minxes! But what do you do about it? Do you say nothing?

VALENTINA: And if I do? Ask them. I scold them all the time; and they hate me for it. They threaten to discredit me with you, so as to oblige you to send me packing. Who knows what lies they make up about me? The servants, whom I try to control, prefer to take their orders from the mistresses, for spite. I am hated by everyone in the house, and only waiting to be turned out of it.

FABRIZIO: Turned out? By whom? I am the master here. I shall send my whole family to the Devil, before I dismiss you. Do your duty, and fear nothing: I give you complete authority over my family. Anyone who fails to show you proper respect will see just what revenge I shall take.

VALENTINA: I lay no claim to anyone's respect. I was born to poverty; your generosity will not make me proud. I shall do my duty, if it is what you ask. I shall treat the young ladies as they should be treated; it is enough if they do not lose their wisdom with their lovers. I know I have never turned to look a handsome youth in the face, and I can boast, during my salad days, of having been the glass of virtue, which is, if not its' own reward, at least rewarded in Heaven.

FABRIZIO: Heaven will the better reward your merits. Here, take this pretty ring. A present.

VALENTINA: For me, signore?

FABRIZIO: Why not?

VALENTINA: It's not something an unmarried girl can wear. If people saw me wearing it, they would say... what they always say - that you are in love with me.

FABRIZIO: They may say what they please.

VALENTINA: Oh, I am too chary of my reputation.

FABRIZIO: Well, if you don't wish... [*Taking back the ring*]

VALENTINA: A master should be able to give his servant a present with impunity.

FABRIZIO: Precisely.

VALENTINA: As an act of obedience, signore, I shall take it.

FABRIZIO: Put it on your finger.

VALENTINA: What would they say *then*?

FABRIZIO: Put it on your finger, and let what will be, be.

VALENTINA: There, it's on. Anyway, I have no great mind to look for a husband. While my master is alive, I'll stay as I am.

FABRIZIO: But before I die, I hope to see you a lady, with a husband.

VALENTINA: You mean you want to abandon me?

FABRIZIO: No, no! Just that I wish... *basta*; Do not oblige me to say any more. One day you will know what I mean.

VALENTINA: You may dispose of me, an obedient girl and a faithful servant.

FABRIZIO: Girl, servant, nothing more?

VALENTINA: Whatever you wish.

FABRIZIO: If, for example, some time...

VALENTINA: Signor, permit me to withdraw. I hear the cook quarrelling in the kitchen, I must see what they are up to below stairs. We shall have time to discuss matters, this evening perhaps. (This ring will do very nicely for Baldissera!) [*She goes out*]

FABRIZIO: Search the world, could I find another woman like her for loyalty? Good judgment? Charm? Discretion? Heaven has sent her for my special consolation. Woe betide me if she were ever to leave my house! I shall make sure of her, I shall make her my wife. My nieces will block my designs, but I shall rid myself of them with all speed: a convent or a husband, but of my choosing. And if ever... which one is this? The elder, it would seem. I shall start with her. Come in, you're just in time.

GIUSEPPINA: [*Entering*] Uncle.

FABRIZIO: Giuseppina.

GIUSEPPINA: Would you know where one might locate Valentina?

FABRIZIO: Valentina is occupied with her own affairs.

GIUSEPPINA: What does that mean? No one's set eyes on her all morning.

FABRIZIO: It means that should you be wanting in respect to her, she will be forced to leave this house.

GIUSEPPINA: You mean Valentina's going?

FABRIZIO: That is what I said.

GIUSEPPINA: Well, let her if she wants to, I don't give a damn.

FABRIZIO: Hey! Hey! What sort of language is that?

GIUSEPPINA: Signor, does it offend you? If she is a relation of yours, I am prepared to respect her, but if she is merely a servant, I shall go on tormenting her.

FABRIZIO: Tormenting her?

GIUSEPPINA: Certainly. Should she give me occasion...

FABRIZIO: Who gives the orders in this house?

GIUSEPPINA: You.

FABRIZIO: Who to?

GIUSEPPINA: Me, among others.

FABRIZIO: Then you must obey.

GIUSEPPINA: My superiors.

FABRIZIO: Your superiors in this house are myself and Valentina.

GIUSEPPINA: The only place she gives orders is the kitchen.

FABRIZIO: She gives orders in my stead to all my family.

GIUSEPPINA: Is she your wife or your daughter?

FABRIZIO: She is my housekeeper.

GIUSEPPINA: But not your householder.

FABRIZIO: She is a woman of great merits.

GIUSEPPINA: Oh, to a degree. There never was a more careful economist. She saves for the master, and puts it on one side for herself. She keeps the food locked away from the servants, and then gets her friends and relations in to share it. She gets up at dawn to see the house is clean, then gets on with her own business with her lover.

FABRIZIO: You have a wicked, wicked tongue! I know why you talk like that, but she is incapable of such iniquities.

GIUSEPPINA: I could prove the truth.

FABRIZIO: The truth is this. Choose how you wish to live.

GIUSEPPINA: I wish to get married.

FABRIZIO: I have a husband for you.

GIUSEPPINA: Young?

FABRIZIO: Sixty years old.

GIUSEPPINA: Bravo, uncle! I shall, of course, be attending my own wedding in person.

FABRIZIO: That you will.

GIUSEPPINA: And if I find the groom is sixty years old, I shall say a flat No.

FABRIZIO: And I a flat Yes.

GIUSEPPINA: Say it then, and marry him yourself.

FABRIZIO: Pert slut! Either marry him, or take yourself off to a convent.

GIUSEPPINA: An uncle has no legal right to impose such conditions on a niece whose father has arranged her dowry. Let me speak plainly, Signor, for myself and for my sister; living with you here before marriage would not be unpleasant. But we have no wish to remain here under a housekeeper giving herself the saucy, arrogant airs of a mistress. She is leading you by the nose, as you will one day learn. We shall shortly make our choice: and you can stay here in peace and charity, with your housekeeper, who will doubtless be keeping a good deal more than that. [*She goes out with an exaggerated curtsey*]

FABRIZIO: Insolent harpy... why did I not take a stick to her? Speaking of Valentina in that way. But what if...? Ehi, it could not be. The poor child predicted how she would speak to me of her. If these insolent girls display such pride before me, what must they be like to her? "I shall, of course, be attending my own wedding in person!" [*Speaking off in the direction GIUSEPPINA left*] Brass-fronted thing! Impertinence! No shadow of judgment! Lose respect for me, and we shall see an avalanche!

ROSINA: [*Entering unseen by FABRIZIO, who has his back to her*] (Who is my uncle bawling at?)

FABRIZIO: I give the orders here, and if I choose a husband, there is no further argument. In a well-conducted girl, such things are shameful.

ROSINA: Are you speaking to me, or my sister, Uncle?

FABRIZIO: [*Turning as he hears her*] Both, if necessary, I presume.

ROSINA: I am not to blame in this: it's Giuseppina.

FABRIZIO: What has the wretched girl done now?

ROSINA: Are you angry?

FABRIZIO: My bile is choking me.

ROSINA: In that case, I shan't say another word.

FABRIZIO: Come now, the fit is passed.

ROSINA: When I see you angry, I go all cold and stiff.

FABRIZIO: Come now, speak up, Rosina, I am not angry any more.

ROSINA: Will you shout at me if I tell you?

FABRIZIO: No, I shall be nice to you.

ROSINA: Who told you about the husband?

FABRIZIO: Giuseppina.

ROSINA: And she told me to be quiet! Fine sister, I must say! Very fine! She wants to bring misfortune on me. She was the reason I spoke, quite against my custom, with the young man.

FABRIZIO: Whom?

ROSINA: The signor Ippolito.

FABRIZIO: And who is this Ippolito?

ROSINA: Do you not know?

FABRIZIO: [*Crossly*] No, I do not, *disgraziata*.

ROSINA: There, now you're cross. If you're going to be like that, I shan't tell you.

FABRIZIO: I am calm, I am quiet. (With some effort) You were talking to the signor Ippolito: and your sister?

ROSINA: She was talking too, with Signor Fulgenzio.

FABRIZIO: [*With a trace of anger*] Capital!

ROSINA: [*Showing alarm*] Signore...

FABRIZIO: [*Forcing himself to contain his rage*] I am laughing. Hahaha.

ROSINA: So you should, uncle. She wants to get married, and so do I.

FABRIZIO: [*Beginning to rave*] I can feel it coming...

ROSINA: Uncle, what is it?

FABRIZIO: [*Controlling himself*] Nothing, nothing, continue.

ROSINA: Is something the matter?

FABRIZIO: Wind.

ROSINA: Shall I go away?

FABRIZIO: No, stay. Why did you not ask the advice of the housekeeper, who would have enlightened you?

ROSINA: That is what we decided, to imitate Valentina and find ourselves husbands.

FABRIZIO: A well-brought-up girl like that! I hardly think...

ROSINA: *Sissignore*, just as she found her Baldissera.

FABRIZIO: [*Agitated, containing his anger*] Who is Baldissera?

ROSINA: Her husband.

FABRIZIO: Whose?

ROSINA: Valentina's. He was here talking to her all morning.

FABRIZIO: [*Heated*] What?... Who saw him?

ROSINA: All the servants.

FABRIZIO: [*Furious*] Damnation!!

ROSINA: Are you angry?

FABRIZIO: [*With exaggerated anger*] Quickly, I want to know what he is, and what he is not. Speak!

ROSINA: [*Running off in terror*] Oh, poor me!

FABRIZIO: Ehi, Rosina, Rosina! Off like the wind - leaving me a prey to apprehension. Is it possible Valentina could be so ungrateful as to deceive me in such a manner? No, it's slander. I know her, she could not play me false. If Giuseppina accused her it was from a malicious inclination to ruin her. Rosina is a nitwit; her sister has imposed on her. She said she saw her with her lover, but might it not have been the butcher, the knife-grinder, the man who clears the midden? But even with one of those she might, if he was... oh, really, no, she is not a woman who holds her honour so lightly; I'd go to the stake for that. The servants saw her? They speak from jealousy, they want me to send her away: but I shall send the whole lot of *them* packing, bag and baggage, and my nieces after them. Valentina is a good girl, wise, honest. And if I did find her to be in love with another? Damnation, double damnation! He'd have me to deal with!

□

# ACT TWO

TOGNINO: Signora Valentina?

VALENTINA: What is it, Tognino?

TOGNINO: Something to tell you.

VALENTINA: Let me guess? Those two amiable young ladies have been telling the old man things about me. Am I right?

TOGNINO: They did their bit: I heard everything from in hiding.

VALENTINA: That is what the maid told me; she heard them talking but she didn't quite understand what they were accusing me of.

TOGNINO: They told the master how you were in love and how Baldissera had been here this morning and how you were planning to take the old man by surprise.

VALENTINA: Did he believe it?

TOGNINO: He sent them off with a flea in their ear. But once he was alone, he was shaking all over. I saw it might be matter for you to hope or fear, so I came to tell you - like you told me.

VALENTINA: Yes, Tognino, *caro*, I'm much obliged to you, and you won't find me ungrateful. But do me this favour: find Baldissera and tell him not to come to see me here this evening, but to wait for me at my sister's house.

TOGNINO: I shall serve you every way I can, but I have a favour to ask you as well. I'm in this difficulty with some friends, I'd like to get out of with honour if possible. We have this club we dine at, and I need to pay my score like the others, but not having any money, I don't know what to do, and you're the only one can help me, Valentina.

VALENTINA: Tognino, you are master of all. I shall give you a nice piece of ham, and a bottle of wine, the best.

TOGNINO: But no one in the house must know.

VALENTINA: Who's to know? Who has the keys here?

TOGNINO: And if I could have two napkins, and two covers.

VALENTINA: Two covers? Who for?

TOGNINO: Me and my lady friend.

VALENTINA: You allow ladies there?

TOGNINO: No fun without them.

VALENTINA: One hand washes the other, and both hands wash the face. Do what you can for me, and I'll do the same for you. The master will know nothing, let me alone for that.

TOGNINO: I'll go and find Baldissera.

VALENTINA: Tell him I will be waiting for him this evening at Felicita's, and I love him as much as he loves me. Will you do that?

TOGNINO: With the best will in all the world.

[*He goes out*]

VALENTINA: From the very first day my maxim has been to keep the rest of the servants on my side: if anyone tries to discredit me with the master, I shall have the whole staff to defend me.

FELICITA: [*Off*] Anyone in?

VALENTINA: Who is it?

FELICITA: [*Off*] Sister, are you there?

VALENTINA: My sister Felicita. On the scrounge. Well, I can be generous with other people's goods. Come in, sister. Are you shy or something?

FELICITA: [*Entering*] I was afraid that old harpy of a master might be here.

VALENTINA: How are you, Felicita?

FELICITA: As well as can be expected for a poor widow with not enough to eat.

VALENTINA: You always come here to whine.

FELICITA: Oh, shut... you always make me say the wrong thing. As if you didn't know! No one comes by my door.

VALENTINA: Why don't you work?

FELICITA: At what? If I make a stocking, what do I get for it? With four or five soldi one can amuse oneself mightily!

VALENTINA: You like doing nothing.

FELICITA: Uh, you can talk, mistress of all you can eat and drink. I'd be happy to try to make my fortune too, if I had a master like yours, stupid as a block. But that is how life is. As for all your brave talk! You haven't had to do much, signora, to get to be where you are.

VALENTINA: I work like a dog, and I have never come asking you for bread.

FELICITA: Oh oh, when my no-good husband was alive how many times did you come to fill your belly?

VALENTINA: To do *what*? You know perfectly well I came at your request. I was astonished at your behaviour. Everything you had you'd frittered away: small wonder your husband died of despair.

FELICITA: Certainly: I was delighted. It was nothing to do with you.

VALENTINA: In which case stop bothering me.

FELICITA: Have no fear, madam, you won't be seeing me here again.

VALENTINA: Come or not, I shan't die for that.

FELICITA: After I've given her the run of my house to meet her lover!

VALENTINA: If I occasionally inconvenience you, I'd have thought you might put with it, seeing what I do for you.

FELICITA: Oh, yes, you keep me alive, don't you? A bag of flour every two months.

VALENTINA: And the barrel of wine, forgotten that, have we? And who paid for your shutters to be repaired? When Baldissera comes to eat with us, there's enough left over to feed you for a week.

FELICITA: There! Begrudging me every crust. You'd sooner throw it to a dog.

VALENTINA: How can you say such a thing in all conscience? If my master's cash-box could talk, it would be accusing you of ingratitude.

FELICITA: Don't you talk to me like that, seeing what I've done for you, and for Baldissera.

VALENTINA: He was to come to your house this evening, but he won't be any more, I'll send to let him know.

FELICITA: Baldissera was coming to me this evening?

VALENTINA: I had some pressing business to discuss with him. It would only have needed a quarter of an hour.

FELICITA: You could stay to supper.

VALENTINA: He may possibly have eaten, but I shall not be coming.

FELICITA: Oh, stop this nonsense, and send him over. I shall expect you this evening. I'm thirsty, Valentina. Give me a glass of wine.

VALENTINA: At this hour of the morning?

FELICITA: I don't want water.

VALENTINA: Chocolate, if you like.

FELICITA: Well, if it's there, I'll drink it: though I dearly love wine.

VALENTINA: We've a very good new wine in at the moment.

FELICITA: Sister dear, let me have a bottle to take home.

VALENTINA: Two if you will. This evening Baldissera will be fetching me... Oh, heavens, who's there?

FELICITA: [*Looking offstage*] Baldissera.

VALENTINA: Is he back? That must mean Tognino couldn't find him.

BALDISSERA: [*Entering*] (Damn my ill luck!)

VALENTINA: Didn't you see Tognino?

BALDISSERA: No.

VALENTINA: You look upset. Tell me, what has happened?

BALDISSERA: Nothing, a headache. (That damned, damned Jack)

FELICITA: [*To BALDISSERA*] If you want supper this evening, come early and bring whatever we need.

BALDISSERA: [*To FELICITA*] Who's talking about supper?

VALENTINA: I wanted to see you at my sister's this evening. I sent Tognino to tell you, because there has been such a rumpus here in the house; and the master has started suspecting something.

FELICITA: So you will come to me, once the master has gone to bed.

BALDISSERA: If he so much as speaks to me, I'll fetch him such a blow on the head. I'd slash the face of the first man who smiles; they'd all better watch out for a desperate man.

FELICITA: That one's a devil. Watch out for him, Valentina.

VALENTINA: You're very hot. What is the matter with you this morning?

BALDISSERA: Hot with love. (Damn this gambling)

VALENTINA: Get along, calm down a bit. I am yours, you know that. Go now, Baldissera, if the old man finds you with me, the fat will be in the fire.

BALDISSERA: (Is that a new ring she has on?)

VALENTINA: Come along with me now.

BALDISSERA: I had a chance of buying a ring, at a very good price, a really nice one. If I'd had the necessary, I'd have bought it for you.

VALENTINA: [*Showing hers*] Prettier than this one?

BALDISSERA: Who gave you that?

VALENTINA: The master.

BALDISSERA: Damnation!

VALENTINA: What's all this damnation?

BALDISSERA: You expect me to say nothing and suspect nothing?

VALENTINA: Of whom?

BALDISSERA: I'm not saying anything.

FELICITA: Are you jealous? Then you know the proverb.

VALENTINA: Are you angry with the master giving it to me?

BALDISSERA: No, but wearing it is a little much. If my Valentina really loves me, if she has more esteem for me than for her master, she will leave the ring in my keeping.

VALENTINA: Your Valentina gives it with all her heart to her dear, dearest Baldissera.

FELICITA: You poor stupid girl! You're throwing it into the canal: but that is how life is. Steal from one to throw away on another.

BALDISSERA: [*Aggressively, to FELICITA*] What do you mean by that?

FELICITA: Nothing.

BALDISSERA: I'm getting angry.

VALENTINA: Hush, someone's coming.

FABRIZIO: [*Off*] Valentina!

VALENTINA: Oh, poor me! The master...

BALDISSERA: Find some excuse.

VALENTINA: Make sure he doesn't see you. Hide, quickly.

BALDISSERA: Where?

VALENTINA: In that room there.

FELICITA: What about me?

VALENTINA: You too.

FELICITA: [*Indicating BALDISSERA*] With him?

VALENTINA: Don't make trouble.

FABRIZIO: [*Off*] Valentina!

VALENTINA: Quickly, he's coming up.

FELICITA: [*To BALDISSERA*] Come along, pretty baby.

VALENTINA: Watch your step, Felicita.

FELICITA: [*Going into the room*] Have no fear, sister dear.

BALDISSERA: [*Going into the room*] I'm relying on you. (I must get away and sell this ring)

FABRIZIO: [*Off*] Valentina!!!

VALENTINA: (All the signs assure me Baldissera loves me. Now we shall see whether the old man mentions him; let him say what he likes, I can easily deal with that)

FABRIZIO: [*Entering, somewhat angry*] Aha, found you at last.

VALENTINA: Was there something?

FABRIZIO: You must answer when the master calls you.

VALENTINA: Did you call me?

FABRIZIO: [*Getting angrier*] Three times.

VALENTINA: [*Haughty*] Had I heard you, I should hardly have delayed.

FABRIZIO: You seem to go deaf when there is some intrigue on hand.

VALENTINA: What are you talking of?

FABRIZIO: Signora, be good enough to tell me who came to see you early this morning?

VALENTINA: Who came... who came... how would I know? the builder, the boilerman, the porter, the tailor and the factor.

FABRIZIO: Butchers, bakers and candlestick makers, pah! tell me honestly, were you not visited by one Baldissera?

VALENTINA: Ah, ah, they've told you! That's it, if a dog comes to piss against the wall, it's back to you in seconds. Every word I say, every move I make, someone flies to inform the master. My every action is spied on, and a master who listens to spies only encourages them.

FABRIZIO: Then those spies you so despise have been telling me the truth? Your anger tells me your secret is out.

VALENTINA: Of course. I have reason to be angry: may I not see whom I please? What am I in this house - a chained slave? Am I denied liberty to go about my own business? On such conditions I wouldn't stay with a prince; find yourself a housekeeper, and I'll find myself a master.

FABRIZIO: You see! The moment I open my mouth, it's: Find yourself another housekeeper. I could break my skull.

VALENTINA: (Break your neck as well)

FABRIZIO: Ingrate, liar! Tell me, at once, who is this Baldissera?

VALENTINA: Very well, I *shall* tell you: he is a gentleman, and a modest young man of excellent parts, noble talents, of the very best family.

FABRIZIO: Is he married?

VALENTINA: Signor, no.

FABRIZIO: Why does he come to see you then?

VALENTINA: We have been fond of each other since childhood.

FABRIZIO: You say that to my face? Traitress!

VALENTINA: Cannot two people like each other without your seeing something reprehensible in it?

FABRIZIO: You're not pulling the wool over my eyes.

VALENTINA: How astute, how perceptive! You really want to know why he came to see me?

FABRIZIO: Why?

VALENTINA: He is in love.

FABRIZIO: Damnation take it!

VALENTINA: And what is wrong with that?

FABRIZIO: In his being in love with you?

VALENTINA: Who said anything about me? There is a deal of malice in you. Have you so little faith in my honesty? If all my affections are to be thrown to the winds, better I go away, and suffer in solitude. I hear myself traduced all day long, I am despised by everybody in this house: the suffering I undergo is pointless, a torture of the damned, a continual death.

FABRIZIO: But if you yourself... Of course, I... I always believed... You are condemned out of your own mouth.

VALENTINA: Condemned, signore, by whom? Is a girl a criminal because she tries to find her sister a husband? Poor Felicita, who was left a widow, you know her, she comes here to see me, no one in the world to provide for her, she needs a husband. I knew Baldissera would be right for her, and I finally persuaded him to take her to wife. But her poverty, signor... the poor girl has nothing in the way of dowry. Knowing my master's feeling for me, I was hoping he might give some help there, but to my chagrin I see his heart is not quite what I thought. My loyalty is held in suspicion: honour demands I should leave this house, to beg my distressful bread along with my sister.

FABRIZIO: [*Pacifying*] Valentina!

VALENTINA: [*Pretending grief*] Signore.

FABRIZIO: Is that true?

VALENTINA: [*A trace of anger*] Can you dare doubt?

FABRIZIO: No, I do not doubt you, dearest. I promise I shall do something for your sister. Would a hundred scudi be enough?

VALENTINA: I am a wicked, ungrateful girl. To quarrel with you...

FABRIZIO: I beg your pardon.

VALENTINA: Did you say a hundred scudi?

FABRIZIO: Yes, the offer was sincerely made.

VALENTINA: [*Ambiguously*] That will be a great help to Baldissera.

FABRIZIO: Are you angry with me?

VALENTINA: Have I not cause enough, signore? I sense ever new suspicions rising in your mind: the cause is all those who come here all day long, deafening you with a thousand bits of gossip, speaking ill of me. But if you really loved me, you would match their tone, and send the whole bunch of them to the Devil.

FABRIZIO: I shall, however many they are, I promise. You know I love you, I know it, I am sure of it. The worries I was harbouring, we shall soon put an end to them; any one who speaks ill of you...

VALENTINA: [*With irony*] Here are your nieces now.

GIUSEPPINA: [*Entering with ROSINA*] (Don't be afraid: the scene is bound to go well)

ROSINA: [*To GIUSEPPINA*] (I don't have the courage)

GIUSEPPINA: (I shall do the talking, sister)

FABRIZIO: What affair brings you both here, signorine?

GIUSEPPINA: An affair of some substance, to tell the truth. Is that not so, Rosina?

ROSINA: I didn't think it was so important. My sister wanted me to come, though.

VALENTINA: [*Ironic*] Since the signora has taken such pains to get here, perhaps she should tell us what it is she finds so important.

GIUSEPPINA: The matter, in fact, is not so important to us as it should be to our uncle - and to you.

VALENTINA: To me, signora?

GIUSEPPINA: [*Indicating the room where BALDISSERA is*] To you. It is hardly good manners to leave that man waiting in that room.

FABRIZIO: What's that? What are you saying?

VALENTINA: (Another complication)

GIUSEPPINA: And our uncle, in charity, should leave you free to be with your lover.

FABRIZIO: Explain yourself.

GIUSEPPINA: [*To ROSINA*] Sister?

ROSINA: Oh, no, I'm not saying anything.

VALENTINA: Such secrets! Then I shall speak first: the man in that room is the signor Baldissera.

FABRIZIO: What? A man in hiding?

VALENTINA: Where is the harm in that?

GIUSEPPINA: No harm at all. And she knows the reason why.

VALENTINA: I do indeed, and so does the signor Fabrizio.

FABRIZIO: I know nothing. I only know concealment is a bad sign. If he wishes to marry your sister, why does he hide himself here?

GIUSEPPINA: [*To ROSINA*] (You hear? She's made him think it's her sister's lover)

ROSINA: (I thought she wanted him for herself)

GIUSEPPINA: (So she does, the brass-fronted thing)

VALENTINA: Softly, softly, signora, don't provoke me too far. In the end I am who I am, and I will make you regret it.

FABRIZIO: How can you deny it, the treason is so clear?

VALENTINA: Signor, with your permission. I shall be back in a moment.
[*Goes into the adjoining room*]

FABRIZIO: Niece, I am betrayed. I am a dead man. I want to see her dead, and pay back the wrong done me.

GIUSEPPINA: [*Ironic*] Signore, place your trust in that good, good creature.

ROSINA: If it wouldn't put you in a passion, I could tell you things.

FABRIZIO: Traitress, perfidious! I'd like to butcher her. Did you see that villain lock himself in there?

ROSINA: I didn't actually see him go in.

GIUSEPPINA: We heard him through the wall, and recognised his voice.

FABRIZIO: Talking? Who with? Who is he shut in there with?

GIUSEPPINA: He will tell you himself.

ROSINA: He sounded very desperate.

FABRIZIO: If he... if he... I have every right to kill him.

ROSINA: Oh, for the love of Heaven, don't frighten me.

GIUSEPPINA: Here he is.

[*FABRIZIO flies into a rage*]

ROSINA: [*To GIUSEPPINA*] Hold him!

GIUSEPPINA: Uncle, control yourself...

BALDISSERA: [*Entering*] Someone looking for me?

FABRIZIO: [*Furious, restrained by GIUSEPPINA*] Rascal! Who do you think you are?

BALDISSERA: I am a gentleman.

FABRIZIO: You are a villain, what are you doing here?

BALDISSERA: With your permission, I came to take a wife.

FABRIZIO: You tell me to my face? Where is the slattern?

FELICITA: [*Entering*] A little respect: I am an honest woman.

FABRIZIO: [*Thunderstruck at seeing FELICITA*] Veh!!

GIUSEPPINA: Felicita here?

ROSINA: I didn't know that.

VALENTINA: There, signore, there is the extent of my crime. I should not have presumed to let them get married in this house. But the poor girl, abandoned by everybody, I had to take her in for charity. I should have told you, I know, I was to blame, an omission for which I ask your pardon: but I knew a generous master, who has done me so many benefits, would pardon this slight fault, were it not for the ill-will of two arrogant nieces, united to ruin me: they are right to hate me, since I am not going to involve myself in their affairs. Had I allowed them the freedom to make love as they pleased, they would not now be treating me with such harshness. But my care for the honour of this house keeps me constantly in these two young ladies' bad books. *Pazienza*, I shall go away. Let them be your responsibility. Let them behave as they like with their lovers. I shall lose my position. [*To FELICITA*] And you, sister, will lose a hundred scudi in dowry he promised me. But as long as my dear master can live in peace, let expectations be scattered to the winds. I can say I served him with love and honour. Let us leave, and leave our fate to Heaven to make of it what it will.

ROSINA: (It almost makes me want to cry)

GIUSEPPINA: (Drat her! Affecting tenderness to make her look virtuous)

FABRIZIO: I don't know where I am any more, nor what I should do. To you two minxes, I shall have a good deal to say.

[*ROSINA runs out without saying anything*]

GIUSEPPINA: To me, signore, to me?

FABRIZIO: Get out.

GIUSEPPINA: You think I am like Rosina? You don't know me.

VALENTINA: [*Ironic*] The signorina Giuseppina is a virtuous girl, with a fortunate mind, and a searching intellect.

GIUSEPPINA: You have a ready wit, capable of changing black into white.

VALENTINA: I shall never attain your happy ingenuity of deception.

GIUSEPPINA: One day you will be made to regret your presumption.

FABRIZIO: Hey there! What sort of talk is this?

VALENTINA: Signor, don't be angry. Since I have already resolved to quit this house, the signora will have no further cause to insult me.

FABRIZIO: No, you shall not leave here: I shall not let you, even at the cost of being somewhat premature. You must stay with me; not as a servant but a lady, mistress while I am alive, and after my death as well. [*To GIUSEPPINA*] And you - either you retire to a convent and rot, or you do exactly what I tell you, and obey her.

GIUSEPPINA: Obey a servant?

FABRIZIO: Servant? I am astonished. She is a housekeeper, and my adviser.

GIUSEPPINA: I am not about to suffer this from some common servant slut. Let her go to the Devil and give him orders.

[*She goes out*]

FABRIZIO: Harridan! I could... I know not what.

VALENTINA: Calm now.

FABRIZIO: I can't.

VALENTINA: If only for my sake.

FABRIZIO: Ah yes, for your sake... you can arm and disarm my temper at will. I know you are a good, wise, honourable girl; I know wicked tongues have persecuted you. If you nourish a real affection for your sister, do her that favour I promised you. These hundred scudi are for her, here, in this purse, I give them to you.

VALENTINA: [*Going for the purse*] I am all obligation, signore.

FELICITA: [*Holding her back*] You are not the bride.

BALDISSERA: [*Holding out his hand*] If I am the bridegroom, give them to me, signore, then there will be no argument.

[*As he holds out his hand, FABRIZIO sees the ring on it*]

FABRIZIO: What's this? The ring I gave you on his finger?

VALENTINA: Signor, I lent it to him.

FABRIZIO: Why?

VALENTINA: These two poor creatures hadn't a ring to get married with.

FABRIZIO: But why is the bridegroom wearing it and not the bride?

VALENTINA: Felicita's fingers are rather thin, the ring was a little loose on her. [*To FELICITA*] Isn't that right?

FELICITA: Oh, yes, yes indeed. I have a very delicate hand.

FABRIZIO: Now it has performed its function he could give it back to you.

VALENTINA: Let Felicita wear it for a day or two so she can show it off round the neighbours.

FABRIZIO: If it's too big, she'll lose it.

VALENTINA: She can pad her finger with a plaster. I really want her relatives to see it. Dear master...

FABRIZIO: Let her hold on to it, if it gives you pleasure. Here are the hundred scudi...

[*He holds the purse up. BALDISSERA whips it out of his hand*]

BALDISSERA: Thank you for your generosity.

FABRIZIO: [*To VALENTINA*] He's quick-fingered enough.

VALENTINA: His poverty is his excuse.

FABRIZIO: [*To BALDISSERA*] Be a good husband to her. [*To FELICITA*] And you a good wife. [*To both*] And when it suits you, come into the house. Whatever Valentina wants: she and no other gives orders under this roof. And anyone who does not like it, must just suffer it. Oh, dear girl, you should be turned to gold.

[*He goes out*]

BALDISSERA: Well done, girl.

FELICITA: Well done, sister.

VALENTINA: [*To BALDISSERA*] You won't be jealous about what he said?

BALDISSERA: I'm not as mad as that; I wish purses like this came every day.

FELICITA: [*To BALDISSERA*] I want my share.

BALDISSERA: [*Making to go*] Very well, but we'll split it up somewhere else. Come along. (I'm off to put this on the cards)

VALENTINA: You're leaving, without saying anything?

BALDISSERA: I'm leaving, because I'm afraid of the people in this house. We'll see each other. Goodbye.

[*He goes*]

FELICITA: I want my half! If he thinks he's going to do me out of a farthing, I'll make the Devil's own row.

[*She goes*]

VALENTINA: There, the net effect of the hatred of those two: Baldissera can come and go here as he pleases, and we can shelter behind this pretended marriage. I know the world would condemn me for treason and ingratitude. But that is the nature of the affection felt by housekeepers for their masters.

□

# ACT THREE

GIUSEPPINA: Sister, let us have one thing clear. That insolent woman is too overbold to be borne; and our uncle, blind to her malice, does us an injustice for the sake of a servant.

ROSINA: Really it is a thing one cannot suffer; nobody I talk to can understand. But I have worked out what's going on. Sister, Valentina has bewitched our uncle.

GIUSEPPINA: Bewitched fiddlesticks! I pique myself on being an observer of such things; I know the whole run of her enchantment. Listen, sister, that woman came to this house as a kitchen-maid, oh-so-demure to begin with; standing, eyes downcast, not saying peep. If she chanced to hear a licentious word, she put her face in her apron, making out to be shocked. She performed her duties with keenness and care, put herself to work in the master's quarters: every second, she would appear in front of him with work in her hands. She heard his orders without looking him in the face; if he made a joke, she would smile; when he went out, she'd help him on with his coat, and help him off with it when he came back. Every morning, when he was barely awake, there she was at his bedside with his chocolate; every evening, she'd put him in his dressing-gown, and tell him the day's happenings in the neighbourhood. To stay at his side, she had the patience to play *tresette* with him for a penny a point. A little flattery, a little gossip and a deal of dedication, sufficed to make him fall in love with her. And once she had succeeded in that, she formed the design of becoming the mistress here. Getting bolder by the day, she set the other servants at variance, egging them on, uncovering various disagreements in the family: cunningly mixing truth and lies, she started setting us against each other. Thinking her a woman of judgment, the old man took her from the kitchen, and made her housekeeper. Now she commands in this house more than the master of it: from what he says, he wants to marry her. And the only witchcraft needed for a common slut of a servant to arrive at that is simple female cunning.

ROSINA: Sister, you know so much about it all, I should have thought you capable of doing just as much.

GIUSEPPINA: I am not capable of using similar wiles, but I know about them, and it will be enough to repair their damage. I have told our aunt Dorotea about it all: she will be here shortly, and be privy to our plan. As our mother's sister, she has every right to defend us against our inhuman uncle.

ROSINA: But she is such a hothead, she will start with an uproar, and be at screaming pitch by tonight. Seriously, sister, if she does not moderate her vice this time, it could be a disaster.

GIUSEPPINA: Let be what will be, it has to finish one day.

ROSINA: But if our aunt loses her temper...

GIUSEPPINA: [*Looking off*] Ah, here she is, right on time.

DOROTEA: [*Entering*] Ah, nieces!

GIUSEPPINA: At your service.

DOROTEA: [*Taking a seat*] You well?

ROSINA: At your service.

DOROTEA: Now when are we going to send this slattern packing? Or mark her face for her?

ROSINA: [*To GIUSEPPINA*] I told you so.

GIUSEPPINA: Aunt, we have no means to send her away. The old man won't listen to us.

DOROTEA: Old fool! Not a thought for his reputation! Ingrained vice!

ROSINA: Oh, hush, they will hear!

DOROTEA: [*Rising in fury*] What if they do? I'll say it to his face, if the devil tempts me. And if he continues to mistreat my nieces, I shall know how to send him packing regardless. [*Sits down again*]

GIUSEPPINA: If you do not assist us...

DOROTEA: [*Squirming on her chair*] We shall see such things!

ROSINA: Just don't make such a noise about it.

DOROTEA: Poor little silly! We'll show 'em.

ROSINA: Can't we think of some way... without too much noise...

DOROTEA: You would do better to hold your tongue.

ROSINA: There! My aunt has made me shut up already, and in the end she will do nothing.

DOROTEA: Oh, damnation! [*Getting up*] There, you've made me say a bad word. Of course, with servants, one must proceed with politeness. Whatever we do, "don't make a scene." [*Parodying ROSINA*] Get away with you, such delicacy! It hardly seems possible such people still exist. [*Sits*]

ROSINA: [*Handkerchief to her eyes*] There, she's always putting me down.

GIUSEPPINA: [*To ROSINA*] It's for our own good.

DOROTEA: Aaaah! Is the baby crying, then? Diddums get put down?

ROSINA: [*Leaving in tears*] Everyone makes game of me. I am really unhappy.

DOROTEA: If that was my daughter, I'd give her such a dunt, she'd have the marks for a week.

GIUSEPPINA: If I were she I'd blow my brains out, if I could think where
   to aim; but let us look for a way to cut the knot of this problem.
DOROTEA: Call the woman here; see what she has to say for herself.
GIUSEPPINA: She won't come if I send for her. And even if she does, there
   is no use our using threats and accusations, if the old man defends her.
DOROTEA: Where is the old fool?
GIUSEPPINA: Still out of the house.
DOROTEA: I'll wait for him, I'll have this out with him today.
GIUSEPPINA: But until he gets back, let you and me give some thought
   to the question of getting *me* out of this house.
DOROTEA: Get married.
GIUSEPPINA: How?
DOROTEA: Don't be awkward. It seems they don't know you are in love.
GIUSEPPINA: Aunt, you can help me. But you could stop scolding me all
   the time.
DOROTEA: Oh, oh, taking offense?
GIUSEPPINA: Of course, when I hear...
DOROTEA: You know what I am like. You should bear anything from an
   old aunt who loves you. I cannot moderate my tone. If Rosina had said
   what you did, I'd pity her. But it seems you are even stupider than she
   is. You know very well I love you.
GIUSEPPINA: Yes, aunt dear, that is plain to see. I trust in your love and
   generosity; I will unlock my heart to you. I love Fulgenzio.
DOROTEA: I know. He was at my house this morning. An excellent match,
   he has all the things which go to make a good husband. He should be
   with us any moment.
GIUSEPPINA: Coming here?
DOROTEA: Absolutely.
GIUSEPPINA: By daylight?
DOROTEA: What's that to do with anything?
GIUSEPPINA: If the old man sees him what is he going to say?
DOROTEA: He can say what he likes. I'll support the engagement.
GIUSEPPINA: No, no, for Heaven's sake.
DOROTEA: Pah! Damn fool!
GIUSEPPINA: Who?
DOROTEA: You.
GIUSEPPINA: Thank you so much.
DOROTEA: What the plague! You don't know you're born. What are you
   afraid of?

GIUSEPPINA: That the old man may not...

DOROTEA: Ain't I here?

GIUSEPPINA: It's not enough.

DOROTEA: Niece, I am getting annoyed. When I hear myself contradicted, I confess I could want in respect to my own father. Nevertheless, do not imagine me so scant in judgment as to wish to provoke a disaster in this house. Let Fulgenzio visit you here: if the old man is not in, we can talk. And if Fabrizio *does* catch sight of him, I shall find a pretext. Leave me alone for that, I am on your side. All will turn out well.

GIUSEPPINA: But there is no need for this hurry...

DOROTEA: Stop contradicting me, drat you.

GIUSEPPINA: To avoid doing so, I shall retire, signora.

DOROTEA: Where the devil do you think you're going? Stay here, dammit!

GIUSEPPINA: Are you angry?

DOROTEA: Ain't hidin' the fact, am I? That is how I came into the world. I am like a mother to you: I would drain the blood from my veins to please you. *Cara,* kiss me, I shall do all I should, just don't stop me saying what comes into my head.

GIUSEPPINA: Oh, it makes no matter to me. But it would be a different matter with my uncle. He's quite your match in sudden rages; I don't want all Milan privy to our affairs.

DOROTEA: Come, now, I can control myself...

GIUSEPPINA: Someone's coming! Who is it?

DOROTEA: Signor Fulgenzio.

GIUSEPPINA: So it is.

DOROTEA: Don't be afraid.

GIUSEPPINA: Come in, signore.

FULGENZIO: May I?

DOROTEA: What's the fool afraid of?

FULGENZIO: I wouldn't want to find...

DOROTEA: Come right in, I say, great, solemn owl.

FULGENZIO: Thank you, signora mia.

DOROTEA: For what? Now no one's by to listen, explain yourself to me. If you want to marry Giuseppina, any delay may prove perilous. Either marry her at once, or break it off - at once.

FULGENZIO: There's a time and place for everything.

DOROTEA: Then it's here and now - oh, rats take you!

GIUSEPPINA: *Caro signor*, my aunt bears you no ill-will. You know who prevails over my uncle's mind; the audacious Valentina, and because he will not give his niece a dowry, her marriage will be blighted, and she will be constrained...

DOROTEA: Forced! Forced to her desperation to be shut up in four walls. And if you've any thought of delaying in lending her your aid, you'd best go be kissed by a bear.

FULGENZIO: Signora, I am not made of stone. Let me think about this.

DOROTEA: Poor mameluke! There she is - young, beautiful, rich, well-bred, well-read, she loves you, she wants to be your wife, you even showed signs of wanting to marry her yourself, and you want to *think*? Ugh, go roast yourself. You're no better than a slave in a seraglio.

FULGENZIO: I shall go without having explained myself at all, as far as I can see, if you're going to be the only one to talk.

DOROTEA: Indeed? And if I hadn't spoken out?

GIUSEPPINA: Aunt, let us hear what he has to say.

DOROTEA: Speak up, then; wasn't it I who brought you here?

FULGENZIO: I am ready to marry her.

DOROTEA: Right away, then...

FULGENZIO: Ah, now...

DOROTEA: Oh, I have black forebodings about you, my son.

FULGENZIO: For why?

DOROTEA: I just have.

FULGENZIO: Before the marriage can be concluded should not a contract be drawn up?

DOROTEA: Go on, go on, waste all your time in excuses; you can be married to her in the intervals between.

FULGENZIO: The uncle would not be so perfidious as to deny his niece the right to a third part of her dowry?

DOROTEA: I see you are one of those lovers who are looking for money. You know the fruit of avarice? You will lose dowry, girl and all. I thought you were of a different character. Run along: I perceive you to be a brute.

FULGENZIO: In that case, I feel I should withdraw. *Servo di lor signore.*

DOROTEA: Pity your father didn't feel the same. *Serva, padron mio.*

GIUSEPPINA: Stop, signor! let me too say a word. My aunt's temper is like to ruin my affairs. If needs must, I can shout just as loud as she; nor, at need, am I afraid of anything. My uncle wishes to marry me off to someone of his choice, disposing of my heart, which I have disposed of elsewhere. And where my satisfaction is concerned, I shall brook no opposition. [*DOROTEA makes a move to interrupt*] No, aunt, allow me to speak. Fulgenzio is right to respect convention, and obtain my uncle's permission for this marriage, and to regulate matters with a contract. But that she-devil will do everything in her power to see nothing happens, or if it does, it will be so far in the future, I shall be dead well before it is realised. The state in which I find myself determines me: my consolation depends on you alone. If it is true you love me, leave all doubts aside.

DOROTEA: And if you don't, you are a degenerate dishclout of a lover.

GIUSEPPINA: Was an added insult absolutely necessary then?

DOROTEA: Can't finish a letter properly without a compliment or two.

FULGENZIO: [*To GIUSEPPINA*] I understand, signora, and as witness of my love, I undertake to give you my hand whenever you please.

DOROTEA: Including now?

FULGENZIO: Including now.

DOROTEA: Saying yes where we said no before?

FULGENZIO: What I did not know before I have now from her own lips.

DOROTEA: No, really, now, unless you're an utter dunderhead, didn't I tell you too? Why act as if you were deaf?

FULGENZIO: Signora Dorotea, when you talk to me like that, deafness would be for me the happier state.

DOROTEA: (Plague take you!)

FULGENZIO: I would give you my hand now, but this lady...

DOROTEA: Listen to the villain! Wearing myself out to finish what I started, and another toad hops out of his ugly mouth. Think an honest girl would allow such a thing without the presence of a single relative? I am her aunt, signore; pray be good enough to give her your hand in my presence.

FULGENZIO: (Such a way with words!)

GIUSEPPINA: Fulgenzio, if you love me, let us make haste, I beg of you.

FULGENZIO: I shall do as you desire.

VALENTINA: [*Entering*] *Serva di lor signori.*

GIUSEPPINA: Well, what do you want?

DOROTEA: No one here sent for you; take yourself off.

VALENTINA: *Signore mie*, forgive me, I came for your good. To inform you that the master is on his way here.

GIUSEPPINA: (Oh, poor me!)

DOROTEA: What is that to us? We lump the master and his adviser together.

VALENTINA: Always a pleasure to see this lady! Her heart is always happy, her face always serene. Such salty humour!

DOROTEA: And you awaken in me the effects of an emetic.

VALENTINA: Better and better.

DOROTEA: I place all my honour in my plain speaking.

FULGENZIO: Signora Dorotea, if you wish, I shall take my leave.

DOROTEA: I shall stay for a little; run along, cousin.

VALENTINA: The gentleman is your cousin?

DOROTEA: My husband's.

VALENTINA: [*Ironic*] How fortunate to have a cousin as accomplished as that.

DOROTEA: What do you mean by that? Fulgenzio is a relative of mine. And if you're suspecting... what I'm suspecting you're suspecting, you're a brass-fronted hussy.

VALENTINA:Suspect? Signora, suspicion is no vice of mine; even if your becoming so heated might give rise to it. On the contrary, it makes me want to laugh: why avoid me, where I can do some good? If my young mistress wants to get married, why so loath to confide in me? Does she think me her enemy? That makes no sense. Were I proud and ambitious to the point of wanting to marry my master, to set myself against her marriage would not be a good idea; were I swayed by self-interest, would I not wish to be alone in this house? Are they afraid I shall oppose their marriages to save my master the expense of their dowries? Even were I capable of such malice, have they not the means to get justice for themselves? If the young ladies had a scrap more confidence in me, they would have been well married by now. Even now, if they would trust me, they'd see what I could do.

FULGENZIO: (Sounds as if the girl's speaking sincerely enough)

GIUSEPPINA: (What do you say, aunt? Shall we trust her?)

DOROTEA: (In the end of the day, what harm can it do?)

GIUSEPPINA: If you had behaved a little more gently with us, I'm sure we would have conceived some affection for you. And if you will engage to work for our wishes, I'm sure we will be able to do something for your good.

VALENTINA: You see, signora? If you had taken my advice you would not have got yourself into this maze. You let your lover come to your apartment, and now your uncle is giving you as a chattel to another.

GIUSEPPINA: Who does he want me to marry?

VALENTINA: Pasquale Monferrato.

DOROTEA: That bedizened old thrombus? I'd flay him alive!

VALENTINA: [*Hearing FABRIZIO approaching*] Here he comes.

GIUSEPPINA: What shall we do?

FULGENZIO: Should I go?

VALENTINA: I don't advise you to go that way.

FULGENZIO: Think of something.

VALENTINA: Hide in that room.

FULGENZIO: And then?

VALENTINA: Let me handle things.

GIUSEPPINA: We trust in you.

DOROTEA: [*Pushing FULGENZIO into the other room*] Out, idiot!

FULGENZIO: [*Going in*] Much obliged.

VALENTINA: (You will be)

GIUSEPPINA: Valentina, I trust you.

VALENTINA: Yes, just do that.

DOROTEA: Don't betray us.

VALENTINA: Oh, you may be sure of that.

FABRIZIO: [*Entering*] Where the devil are you?

GIUSEPPINA: We are here, uncle.

FABRIZIO: [*Angrily, to DOROTEA*] You too, signora?

DOROTEA: Certainly, I am.

FABRIZIO: Could you not possibly do us the favour of going away?

DOROTEA: What appalling manners! Stupid old relic!

FABRIZIO: She-devil!

DOROTEA: Heretic!

FABRIZIO: The boldness!

DOROTEA: The sauce!

FABRIZIO: The gall!

DOROTEA: The crust!

VALENTINA: [*With authority*] What is this turmoil? [*To FABRIZIO*] Be quiet, signore.

FABRIZIO: That woman is an insolent harridan.

VALENTINA: I don't want any shouting.

FABRIZIO: Must I bear it? *Pazienza!*

GIUSEPPINA: (A cunning woman always has power to soothe the savage breast)

FABRIZIO: Niece, I was looking for you. I came to tell you I have just married you off. You will be pleased to know you may finally leave this house, with your husband, the signor Pasquale.

DOROTEA: That cadaver?

FABRIZIO: She will accept him.

DOROTEA: She doesn't want him.

FABRIZIO: She shall take him, by this hand.

DOROTEA: She shall not, by this fist.

FABRIZIO: Who gives the orders here?

VALENTINA: Signore, forgive me, one should not be overbearing with young girls. She wishes to get married to the man of her choice. An uncle, if he is a gentleman, should suffer that in silence. She has another husband ready to marry her.

FABRIZIO: And who might that be?

VALENTINA: Fulgenzio, who is hiding in there.

FABRIZIO: What!

GIUSEPPINA: What are you saying?

DOROTEA: Is this your promise?

VALENTINA: I thought it for the best.

DOROTEA: You deserve a good cut of the tawse.

VALENTINA: Softly, signora, no need of such talk to me. I served her as she served me with Baldissera. If she acted from zeal, expect the same from me; if she acted from spite, I acted from revenge. I have justified myself with my master; let her make shift to do so, if she can. And if my plans have turned out sour for her, let her wit teach her not to provoke me.

GIUSEPPINA: Traitress!

DOROTEA: Shameless!

FABRIZIO: [At the door where FULGENZIO is] Come out of that room!

FULGENZIO: [Emerging] Signor, less uproar. I leave these walls, but only because you are master of them. [To VALENTINA, as he goes] But you, perfidious woman, you will pay for this.

FABRIZIO: A dog baying at the moon.

GIUSEPPINA: [To FABRIZIO] Signor, I ask your pardon. [To VALENTINA, as she goes] Traitress, one day I will show you who I am.

DOROTEA: [To VALENTINA] I shan't forget this.

FABRIZIO: Don't frighten us.

DOROTEA: [Leaving] Dreadful old man!

VALENTINA: You hear? Because I acted out of love for you, I must suffer a thousand punishments. They all would see me dead.

FABRIZIO: Have no fear of them. They will find out who I am.

VALENTINA: With Giuseppina in the house I shall not draw a quiet breath.

FABRIZIO: What am I to do with her?

VALENTINA: Put her in a convent.

FABRIZIO: At once, willingly or by force. They will soon find out who I am and who I am not. They will find out Valentina commands in this house. Today... I mean today... you shall be my wife. [He goes]

VALENTINA: That's of no great matter to me: come what may, I mean to marry Baldissera. But before I reveal the love that is burning me up inside, I mean to provide myself with everything I need. Of the two sisters, the first has been punished, the second wants my assistance to get married. Ippolito loves her, I shall come to an understanding with him - and pocket a prodigious tip. In this world, those who cut a figure are those who know how to use cunning and imposture. True, the ground can sometimes produce earthquakes, but if luck is on my side, I may hope for a happy ending.

□

# ACT FOUR

FELICITA: A right fool I'd be to keep my mouth shut. A hundred scudi, and you give me a rotten six!

BALDISSERA: You call six scudi nothing? A lot you did to earn them, I must say.

FELICITA: And a deal of sweat they cost you, I don't think. Give me the rest, or I'll scream the place down.

BALDISSERA: May I be massacred if you get another doit. I'm sorry now I gave you what I did.

FELICITA: There, if you want them.

BALDISSERA: Just give them to me.

FELICITA: You brigand! Will you be gambling those away too?

BALDISSERA: Gamble? Me?

FELICITA: Poor baby! Of course, he never goes near a table. Why else does he never have a penny piece in his pocket?

BALDISSERA: Who told you?

FELICITA: Half a dozen people, and I've seen you coming out of the casino myself. If Valentina were to find out...

BALDISSERA: Just take care she doesn't find out from you.

FELICITA: What will you give me?

BALDISSERA: Anything you want.

FELICITA: I want another ten scudi. It's called commission.

BALDISSERA: Another ten then. It's called blackmail.

FELICITA: Show me.

BALDISSERA: Now?

FELICITA: This minute.

BALDISSERA: Bye and bye.

FELICITA: Goodbye and goodbye: you lost them gambling.

BALDISSERA: You want to ruin me. Please, Felicita, please don't tell Valentina.

FELICITA: If I don't get ten scudi, I can't guarantee to keep quiet.

BALDISSERA: But where can I lay hands on them?

FELICITA: Give me the ring as a pledge.

BALDISSERA: Ring?

FELICITA: The ring she gave you.

BALDISSERA: Valentina?

FELICITA: Precisely. [*BALDISSERA is silent*] Sold?

BALDISSERA: Pawned.

FELICITA: To gamble with.

BALDISSERA: My luck has to change soon.

FELICITA: My poor sister! She will be destitute. I must warn her.

BALDISSERA: No! For pity's sake.

FELICITA: For pity's sake, I should keep quiet? Not so easy. Charity, brother, begins right here at home. If Valentina is to be made wretched on account of you, what ought I to do?

BALDISSERA: Felicita, I swear, I won't gamble any more. Arrange for Valentina to marry me at once; I'll be a good friend to you, and a good relation - and I'll throw in three hundred scudi as a consideration.

FELICITA: Can I have that in writing?

BALDISSERA: Signed, if you like.

FELICITA: I want it witnessed by a notary public.

BALDISSERA: Whatever ceremony you wish.

FELICITA: [*Drawing up a little table with writing materials*] Here's everything we need. Draw up the deed.

BALDISSERA: Right away, at your service.

FELICITA: Do it properly.

BALDISSERA: [*Writing*] (In a case like this I'd sign away a thousand. Always find ways and means to get out of it later on. If my luck changes, I may still find some way to get it back again).

FELICITA: (I make no predictions about what's going to happen. I'll put these three hundred scudi to one side. If my luck changes, I may still find someone to get married to again)

BALDISSERA: What's Valentina going to say?

FELICITA: There will be no argument. Pay the notary for a consultation at home, and two gratuities. If I can persuade her to marry you, our agreement can be extended to cover the marriage.

BALDISSERA: You've got a cunning head on your shoulders. Just see the marriage arranged for today. I'll call in at the notary's and be back as soon as I can. You're a worthy sister for Valentina! [*He goes out*]

FELICITA: Not even to Valentina do I yield in the matter of *savoir-faire*. We are daughters of a mother who could teach us both something. Natural aptitude has perfected the example she gave us.

VALENTINA: [*Entering*] What are you doing here, sister?

FELICITA: Waiting for you, for the last hour.

VALENTINA: I was with the old man.

FELICITA: Where is he?

VALENTINA: In bed. He sleeps for at least two hours every afternoon.

FELICITA: In which case you are free for two hours.

VALENTINA: Unless some accident wakes him sooner. I think the devil is in this house. The two sisters are sulking in their rooms; the old man didn't want them in his sight. And the eldest, who is obsessed against me, is being dragged off to a convent tomorrow.

FELICITA: A good thing for you. Get rid of the proud, artful thing. Why don't you arrange for the other one to be shut up too?

VALENTINA: Rosina's a good enough girl; without her sister I've found her quite human. She is in love with an innocent young man, name of Ippolito. He's coming to see me soon: I want to marry her off, out of spite, for the things the other one's said about me. Let her have the mortification of seeing her younger sister married first.

FELICITA: On which subject, sister, when are you getting married?

VALENTINA: There's time.

FELICITA: Ehi, you ought to make haste.

VALENTINA: I'm not mad enough to do it yet; once I'm married, my affair with the master will be over: and before that happens, I want to see him make a will in my favour, and after his death I can at least be sure of my position. Meanwhile, Baldissera will have to exercise a little restraint.

FELICITA: Poor Baldissera! It's not as if he had any vices.

VALENTINA: Gambling?

FELICITA: Given it up. I know for a fact.

VALENTINA: Really? You relieve me.

FELICITA: Morning, noon and night he does nothing but sigh for his Valentina. Why not put him out of his misery?

VALENTINA: I would if I could. But if I leave here, what becomes of us?

FELICITA: Could you not marry him, and have him come to live here?

VALENTINA: What?

FELICITA: Come, you're a woman who prides herself on her wit. Didn't the old man think just now I was married to Baldissera?

VALENTINA: True, he swallowed that.

FELICITA: Didn't he give the both of us permission to come and go as we pleased, in the house, day or night?

VALENTINA: What would he not do for me?

FELICITA: Then for you he can give us permission to come and stay in the house. By day, he can go on thinking him my husband, and the old fool won't see who he sleeps with by night.

VALENTINA: My heavens, the trick could work. Let us arrange the wedding.

FELICITA: We'll do it immediately. Who's that knocking?

VALENTINA: [*Looking out of the window*] Rosina's lover. Go and let him in. Tell him to be quiet, the other one mustn't hear him, and have him come to me here.

FELICITA: Will she be coming?

VALENTINA: Yes, I warned her.

FELICITA: But if Baldissera comes...

VALENTINA: Just do it.

FELICITA: [*Going*] Sister, you won't regret doing what I advise. (If he lets me into the house, I might even get enough to eat)

VALENTINA: (*Caro il mio* Baldissera, so you do love me a little. I am so glad you have given up gambling)

IPPOLITO: [*Off*] Can I come in?

VALENTINA: Yes, do.

IPPOLITO: [*His head round the door*] I'm sorry.

VALENTINA: Please.

IPPOLITO: I wouldn't like to...

VALENTINA: Come on in.

IPPOLITO: I don't know if you will understand me...

VALENTINA: What do you mean?

IPPOLITO: I'm sorry.

VALENTINA: Say it.

IPPOLITO: There wouldn't be any danger of a beating?

VALENTINA: Signor, I am astonished. I am a woman of judgment.

IPPOLITO: I don't doubt it. I'm sorry.

VALENTINA: Then come in...

IPPOLITO: Where is signor Fabrizio?

VALENTINA: Asleep.

IPPOLITO: Asleep?

VALENTINA: I want this business hurried along.

IPPOLITO: Speak quietly.

VALENTINA: Why?

IPPOLITO: I wouldn't want to wake him.

VALENTINA: Are you so frightened of him?

IPPOLITO: Oho, you are in error.

VALENTINA: [*Louder*] In which case, signor Ippolito...

IPPOLITO: We mustn't make a noise. How is Rosina?

VALENTINA: You will see her soon.

IPPOLITO: Where?

VALENTINA: Here.

IPPOLITO: I'd better go.

VALENTINA: Don't you want to see her?

IPPOLITO: Yes and no... I know I've talked to her, but I've never seen her in daylight.

VALENTINA: Well?

IPPOLITO: Well, if she comes in here, and sees me, I'm sorry, but I might be a bit shy.

VALENTINA: Do you think you're so ugly?

IPPOLITO: Ugly? Signora no. I've seen myself in the mirror, I know I'm not ugly. But I never made love to anyone in all my life, and I feel a bit backward doing it for the first time. I'm sorry.

VALENTINA: How old are you?

IPPOLITO: Twenty three... and a half.

VALENTINA: And for twenty three years... and a half, you have had so little experience in love?

IPPOLITO: The fact is, while my mother was alive, she kept me away from...

VALENTINA: Women?

IPPOLITO: Mmm... Once I made a joke to a lady, and my mother gave me a slap I can still feel.

VALENTINA: Do you want to get married?

IPPOLITO: Yes, I most certainly do.

VALENTINA: Here is the young lady now.

IPPOLITO: I'll take my leave.

VALENTINA: (Masterpieces like him are meat and drink to me)

ROSINA: [*Entering*] Who wants me?

VALENTINA: I do.

IPPOLITO: [*Pleased with ROSINA's looks, but withdrawing shyly*] Oh, she's beautiful!

ROSINA: [*To VALENTINA*] Who is that?

VALENTINA: Ippolito.

ROSINA: Really?

VALENTINA: Don't you know him?

ROSINA: (He's handsome)

VALENTINA: But I know you have spoken together.

ROSINA: Never by daylight.

VALENTINA: And how do you like him now?

ROSINA: Even more.

VALENTINA: Aren't you going to greet him?

ROSINA: *Schiava.*
IPPOLITO: *La sua.*
VALENTINA: Go on, say something.
ROSINA: Like what?
IPPOLITO: I don't know.
VALENTINA: Then answer me, at least. Do you love Rosina? [*IPPOLITO laughs*] What is that supposed to mean? Explain yourself; do you love her? [*IPPOLITO nods*] Tell me in words.
IPPOLITO: [*Aside to VALENTINA*] I'm shy.
VALENTINA: And I am stupid to bother with you.
IPPOLITO: Oh, don't be angry.
VALENTINA: Do you love her, yes or no?
IPPOLITO: Yes, didn't I tell you so?
VALENTINA: Now you tell me, I know. And you, *signora mia,* do you want to say it to me?
ROSINA: Do you have to make me blush? Didn't I tell you in my room?
VALENTINA: Say it again here. Do you love him or do you not?
ROSINA: I love him.
IPPOLITO: [*Jumping for joy*] She said yes!
VALENTINA: Do you want to marry her?
IPPOLITO: Me?
VALENTINA: Yes, you. Do you want her?
IPPOLITO: Is the Signor Fabrizio asleep?
VALENTINA: Yes. What are you afraid of? Well?
IPPOLITO: I'll say what she says.
VALENTINA: [*To ROSINA*] And what do you say?
ROSINA: Yes.
IPPOLITO: [*A-tremble for joy*] Is signor Fabrizio coming?
VALENTINA: No, he is not, and if he does, he will not contradict anything. You will be married today: your uncle will give you the dowry which is legally due to the married niece. [*To IPPOLITO*] On which subject, we will need to have a little talk.
IPPOLITO: [*Blushing*] What have I to do with a dowry? I'm not interested in dowries. I'm happy to be... I'm sorry.
VALENTINA: Why do you stop?
IPPOLITO: I meant I was happy just to be married to this ... lady.
VALENTINA: [*To ROSINA*] You, go into the next room. [*To IPPOLITO*] And you, go and wait in the café next door.
IPPOLITO: Do it quickly.

ROSINA: Don't keep me on tenterhooks.

IPPOLITO: I am on the rack.

ROSINA: I am in chains.

VALENTINA: You hear how love makes monkeys of you. Will it be too
   much to ask you to say "yes"?

IPPOLITO: I go.

ROSINA: I shall withdraw.

IPPOLITO: (What torment!)

ROSINA: (What martyrdom!)

IPPOLITO: Farewell, my dearest wife.

ROSINA: Farewell, my handsome husband.

   [*They go out in opposite directions*]

VALENTINA: Carrying on like organ-grinders: one penny to start them
   off, and three to stop them.

FELICITA: [*Entering*] How is the business going?

VALENTINA: Well: this evening it will be concluded.

FELICITA: Baldissera is coming.

VALENTINA: Let him: we can talk of our business now.

BALDISSERA: [*Entering with the NOTARY*] Come in, signor Notary. (Oh,
   Valentina's here)

FELICITA: Is this the notary?

NOTARY: It is, signora, it is.

BALDISSERA: [*To FELICITA*] What shall we do?

FELICITA: (Hush!) Listen, sister, if I have chosen an arbitrator, don't take
   it amiss. Hearing that marriage would not entirely displease you, I told
   Baldissera to bring a notary. Was I wrong?

VALENTINA: Just *when* did you tell him?

FELICITA: Just now: after I went to call your niece.

VALENTINA: What did Baldissera say?

FELICITA: He was delighted. Come in, signor Notary, the parties are all
   here present. They want to get married. Don't you?

BALDISSERA: If Valentina agrees.

VALENTINA: I am as content as I could be.

FELICITA: [*To the NOTARY*] Start writing, start writing: make yourself
   comfortable, *vossignoria illustrissima*.

NOTARY: [*Sitting and starting to write*] May I have the bride?

VALENTINA: I am she.

NOTARY: Tell me how I should refer to you in the document.

   [*VALENTINA speaks softly to the NOTARY, who continues to write*]

FELICITA: [*Aside, to BALDISSERA*] (What do you say, Baldissera? Do I deserve the three hundred scudi? I want four)

BALDISSERA: (Whatever you want)

FELICITA: (Furthermore, you know we can stay here, and get board as well)

BALDISSERA: (How's the old man not going to be jealous?)

FELICITA: (He thinks you're mine...)

NOTARY: Can I now have the bridegroom?

[*BALDISSERA goes to the NOTARY, and appears to be giving him his opinion*]

VALENTINA: Just thinking about this makes me weak at the knees.

FELICITA: When it's done, don't think about it any more.

VALENTINA: If the old man finds out, it will be a disaster.

FELICITA: It's up to you to be discreet.

VALENTINA: It's not easy pretending to be a young girl with your husband standing next to you.

FELICITA: Stuff! You want to be with your husband every hour of the day? We have to take a little trouble, to get what we want in this world.

VALENTINA: But there must come a time when I won't be able to keep it secret any longer.

FABRIZIO: [*Entering*] Just what is going on?

VALENTINA: (O the devil! the master)

BALDISSERA: (The fat is now truly in the fire)

FELICITA: (Invent something)

VALENTINA: (All right, all right, I won't lose my head)

FABRIZIO: What is happening, Valentina?

VALENTINA: A marriage contract.

FABRIZIO: For whom, pray?

VALENTINA: For Rosina. The signor Ippolito is coming, he won't be many moments. I spoke to the girl; both are content. I called the notary; he is drawing up the contract; you can see it as soon as he is done. Or have you changed your mind?

FABRIZIO: No, but what has Baldissera to do with such a marriage?

VALENTINA: He is a witness.

FABRIZIO: [*To the NOTARY*] Your servant, signor.

NOTARY: Servant, *padron mio*.

FABRIZIO: With your kind permission, I should like to see that too.

NOTARY: And who are you?

FABRIZIO: Who am I? Some one who doesn't count, it seems! Who am I? That is rich! The uncle of the bride!

VALENTINA: [*Taking up the paper from the table*] Come, don't upset yourself. Here is the deed; take it and read it. Where are your glasses? ehi! it will be two hours before you find them; I'll read it, signore - if the notary is agreeable? - we can read it quietly together. This day etcetera of the year one thousand etcetera, by these presents etcetera by the authority vested etcetera, Rosa Panfili, niece of Fabrizio Panfili, undertakes to marry Ippolito Moschin, formerly Maurizio. The uncle of the bride aforementioned undertakes to give ten thousand scudi in dowry, which ten thousand scudi shall be assured by an agreement with the bridegroom, entailing his inherited goods. And in obligation etcetera by me, and protesting etcetera, by these presents etcetera by me notary etcetera, how does that seem to you?

FABRIZIO: How does it seem to you?

VALENTINA: Excellent.

FABRIZIO: If you are happy, I am very happy.

VALENTINA: Then if you are agreeable, just sign the contract.

FABRIZIO: Willingly. "I, Fabrizio de' Panfili, with my own hand, approve and confirm..." [*Signing*] Thank you, signor Notary.

NOTARY: Signor, my respects.

VALENTINA: [*To FABRIZIO*] Give him his fee.

FABRIZIO: There, a zecchino for you.

NOTARY: [*Making to go*] Much obliged. Forgive my not recognising you.

FABRIZIO: [*Saluting*] Signore.

FELICITA: [*Aside to the NOTARY*] (Wait for me downstairs, I have something to say to you too)

NOTARY: [*Going*] (At your service)

VALENTINA: I shall hold on to this document.

FABRIZIO: Give it to me.

VALENTINA: No, no, it will be safer in my chest.

FABRIZIO: Where is Rosina?

VALENTINA: You will see her soon. Now I must talk to you about something else.

FABRIZIO: What is it?

VALENTINA: I wanted to ask you...

FABRIZIO: Ask me? What are you saying? *Command* me.

VALENTINA: So that I shall not be alone all my life, I want my sister Felicita and her husband to come and keep me company. They would be a great help to me, with a hundred and one things. All they need is a room and a bed.

FABRIZIO: Beneath this roof, you command and you alone. Let them come, if that will please you. Whatever you like, you don't need to ask.

VALENTINA: I am all obligation.

FABRIZIO: Why all this ceremony?

VALENTINA: All this generosity...

FABRIZIO: [Going] Stop this, before it drives me mad.

FELICITA: Brava, brava, sister. All goes well, I knew it. [Aside to BALDIS-SERA, and leaving] (And you and I will go and sign the deed at the notary's)

VALENTINA: What do you think, Baldissera?

BALDISSERA: [Going] What are women not capable of in this world!

VALENTINA: Oh, women, women are cunning enough, in all conscience. But not many could hold a candle to me. If the end of this matches the beginning, I, of all women, shall deserve a regular coronation.

□

# ACT FIVE

GIUSEPPINA: Now, aunt, the old man has gone out. We can speak without fear.

DOROTEA: Fear? Of whom, pray? I have come here resolved to provoke a right royal catastrophe. Could there be a more traitorous, a more raging, furious hound? I never saw the like in the animal creation. Chase you into a nunnery? An uncle use such overbearing means to his niece? And for whom, rat him! A servant-girl, an insolent jumped-up slut, the idea!

GIUSEPPINA: This wild, unruly talk, and where does it get us? We waste time in chatter, and time flies; aunt dear, screaming is not enough. I want deeds.

DOROTEA: Be off with you, you are all very vague. Nothing is left but to fetch the old monument a blow on the head.

GIUSEPPINA: Bodily harm, signora, is for the lower classes. If there is nothing else you can think of...

DOROTEA: Well, if it ain't to your taste, stop bothering me with it.

GIUSEPPINA: Could not one rather...?

DOROTEA: You make objections to every blessed thing. That way you will lose both baby *and* bathwater.

GIUSEPPINA: In my house, surely...

DOROTEA: Always the same.

GIUSEPPINA: I can speak, and arrange...

DOROTEA: Go on! Play the professor!

GIUSEPPINA: The way in which...

DOROTEA: I can't abide her.

GIUSEPPINA: [*Heatedly*] Will you let me speak!

DOROTEA: What did you wish to say?

GIUSEPPINA: I wish to say, signora, that if you are interested in my case, go to the Governor and accuse my uncle. Say that the malice occasioned by a servant's deception has made him do his niece an injustice, and that the only remedy is to present a memorial to the courts, demand justice, do what needs to be done to get me out of this house, and not waste time and breath in swearing and shouting.

DOROTEA: [*Placidly*] Why such heat? Speak lovingly, as I do. You say well, we can have recourse to the Governor; draw up a memorial and present it to the Courts.

GIUSEPPINA: But we need protection.

DOROTEA: Protection! Fiddlesticks! Come along. I've a bone to pick with that old image. I want him to pay back everything his brother left him, and account for every penny he has consumed: and I shall invoke the full rigour of the Law to do it, if it is the last thing I do.

GIUSEPPINA: And while you are litigating, he will go on maltreating me.

DOROTEA: What the devil more do you need to make you happy?

GIUSEPPINA: Justice, protection and a way out of here.

DOROTEA: Plague take you, justice you shall have.

GIUSEPPINA: But if you...

DOROTEA: But if I what...

FULGENZIO: [*Entering*] With permission, signore? Knowing signor Fabrizio had left the house, I took the liberty of paying you a visit, to ascertain the truth about a certain fact.

GIUSEPPINA: Certainly: my uncle has decided to put me into a convent.

DOROTEA: But we shall block his path with a lawsuit.

FULGENZIO: Never mind that. What I wish to know is, how is it your sister has got married to Ippolito?

GIUSEPPINA: Rosina?

FULGENZIO: *Sissignora.*

DOROTEA: Married?

FULGENZIO: Did you not know?

DOROTEA: I did not, nor do I believe it.

GIUSEPPINA: Signor, you are deceived.

FULGENZIO: How can I be deceived, when the old man is sitting in the corner café telling all his acquaintance about it? He named the notary who drew up the contract, and he is spending quite a lot in celebration.

GIUSEPPINA: This is all new to me.

DOROTEA: You must be dreaming.

FULGENZIO: I tell you it is the truth.

DOROTEA: [*Going out*] Rosa! Where is she? Wait!

FULGENZIO: This would be a great wrong to an elder sister.

GIUSEPPINA: Who could have given the ignorant thing leave?

FULGENZIO: I would be no great matter had you yourself agreed to it. What sort of girl would she be not to want to get married?

GIUSEPPINA: Without a word to me?

FULGENZIO: Women take advice when choosing a dress, not a husband.

GIUSEPPINA: I still can't believe it.

FULGENZIO: You'll hear it from her own lips.

GIUSEPPINA: But if she's married, my uncle can have no objection to our...
FULGENZIO: There will be no need for his permission. I have warned the Governor about the whole affair, and he has promised to give you the necessary assistance. In justice, your uncle will have to give you the dowry, if the other dowry has been assigned.
GIUSEPPINA: And is my younger sister to be wed before me?
FULGENZIO: What's done is done.
GIUSEPPINA: Not if I can help it.
FULGENZIO: Here she is now.
GIUSEPPINA: If this is true, she will hear from me.
DOROTEA: [*Entering with ROSINA*] Here she is, the brass-fronted thing, the pert hussy.
GIUSEPPINA: How, sister, without telling me a thing?
ROSINA: Oh, that's very nice! If they want to give him to me, if he says he'll take me, shouldn't I snatch the chance?
GIUSEPPINA: So you *are* married.
ROSINA: Married? I don't know.
FULGENZIO: Didn't you sign the contract?
ROSINA: Contract? Signor no.
GIUSEPPINA: But wasn't the notary here?
ROSINA: He didn't come here for me.
DOROTEA: Did the old man sign it?
ROSINA: My uncle didn't see it.
GIUSEPPINA: Who performed the marriage?
ROSINA: I'll tell you how it was. Valentina called me into the room. Signor Ippolito was here. He asked me if I wanted to be his wife. I was shy at first, hearing him talk like that. But then...
DOROTEA: What did you do?
ROSINA: I said yes.
GIUSEPPINA: And they made the contract?
ROSINA: Nobody made anything.
GIUSEPPINA: Were there witnesses?
ROSINA: There was nobody.
GIUSEPPINA: [*To FULGENZIO*] What was all that about the lawyer? About the contract?
FULGENZIO: Signor Fabrizio said the marriage had happened.
GIUSEPPINA: [*To ROSINA*] You hear?
ROSINA: I don't know anything else. Ippolito went away, and Valentina said he would be my husband.

GIUSEPPINA: Would be? Then he isn't yet. If Ippolito went away, then it is reasonable to assume you are not yet a wife. In which case, Signor Fulgenzio, you misunderstood.

DOROTEA: In my opinion, Fulgenzio is fit to be chained.

FULGENZIO: Do we know, are we quite sure, *signore mie,* that the signora Rosina is speaking the truth?

ROSINA: I don't tell lies.

TOGNINO: [*Entering*] There is a signor Ippolito asking for the mistress.

GIUSEPPINA: Have him come in.

ROSINA: Call Valentina.

TOGNINO: Signora, she has locked herself in her room: I knocked but there was no answer. I think she is asleep. The signor Ippolito wished to speak to her too.

ROSINA: Where is signor Ippolito?

TOGNINO: Here he is coming now.

ROSINA: I shall go.

GIUSEPPINA: Stay where you are.

DOROTEA: [*Derisively, to ROSINA*] The nitwit has woken up, I see.

ROSINA: I'll give you the answer to that when I'm married.

IPPOLITO: [*Enters*] Rosina... oh, lord, so many people! *Servo di tutti.*

GIUSEPPINA: Come in, signor Ippolito.

IPPOLITO: Thank you. An honour.

FULGENZIO: *Amico,* I am relieved. You are married at last.

IPPOLITO: Well, not yet... but I hope...

FULGENZIO: You aren't married?

IPPOLITO: Not married, promised. I have every hope of doing it tomorrow morning.

FULGENZIO: But didn't Malacura the lawyer draw up the contract? Didn't you sign it?

IPPOLITO: I know nothing of that.

GIUSEPPINA: There now, signor Fulgenzio, the whole thing was a fabrication.

DOROTEA: I always said Fulgenzio was next to an idiot.

FULGENZIO: I must go and find that lawyer: I know where his chambers are. I shall be back in a trice, signore, please wait for me.

DOROTEA: Be off with you, blockhead.

FULGENZIO: [*To DOROTEA, as he goes*] If this is true, I shall know how to change things.

IPPOLITO: [*Essaying a joke*] *Cara la mia Rosina!*

GIUSEPPINA: Ehi, a little respect there!

IPPOLITO: Is she not mine?

GIUSEPPINA: Not yet she isn't.

IPPOLITO: [*To ROSINA*] Oh, that lovely face!

GIUSEPPINA: Believe me, signor, you are not likely to be seeing Rosina married before me.

IPPOLITO: Ehi, signora sister-in-law, people marry when they please. I wish you with all my heart peace, health and many children.

DOROTEA: Meanwhile your marriage may be about to go up in smoke.

IPPOLITO: Smoke? For what reason?

ROSINA: I don't believe it.

DOROTEA: It might.

ROSINA: Really?

DOROTEA: I can assure you.

ROSINA: You can't know that.

DOROTEA: Indeed I can, minx!

IPPOLITO: I'm staying here.

GIUSEPPINA: Who organised the whole affair?

IPPOLITO: Valentina, signore.

GIUSEPPINA: Did you speak to my uncle?

IPPOLITO: I haven't seen him yet.

DOROTEA: So marriages are arranged by servants here!

IPPOLITO: I shall die on the spot.

ROSINA: [*To IPPOLITO*] Fear nothing.

IPPOLITO: [*Happily*] You mean that?

ROSINA: I promise.

IPPOLITO: [*Jumps for joy*] Hurrah!

DOROTEA: Oh, be quiet, simpleton!

FULGENZIO: [*As the NOTARY enters*] Here is signor Malacura: he will tell you himself, whether he drew up the contract or not.

NOTARY: Yes, signori, not three hours ago.

FULGENZIO: [*To DOROTEA*] Now am I a blockhead?

DOROTEA: [*To the NOTARY*] Did the parties sign?

NOTARY: Certainly, in their own hands.

DOROTEA: [*To IPPOLITO*] As for you, signor liar... [*To ROSINA*] And you, stupid insolent girl, telling us you knew nothing about it.

ROSINA: [*To NOTARY*] I signed the contract?

IPPOLITO: [*To the NOTARY*] Did I sign it?

NOTARY: Oh my!

GIUSEPPINA: [*To the NOTARY*] These are the parties, are they not?

NOTARY: These? No, they are not.

DOROTEA: Oh, rich!

GIUSEPPINA: Very fine!

FULGENZIO: [*To the NOTARY*] Then who were they?

NOTARY: [*Taking out a notebook*] If I remember correctly ... here, I made a note: "*Valentina Marmita and Baldissera Orzata.*"

GIUSEPPINA: The housekeeper!

DOROTEA: Married her friend.

FULGENZIO: What a curious situation.

DOROTEA: If it is, it's because you're deaf.

FULGENZIO: But if Fabrizio himself...

DOROTEA: And he's blind. Oh, be off with you, you're a half-wit.

FULGENZIO: Signora, that is a little much...

GIUSEPPINA: But how did the old man not fly off the handle? Tell me, signor, did the master know about this?

NOTARY: Most certainly, he put his signature to it.

GIUSEPPINA: Now how in the name of...? Does the contract mention a dowry?

NOTARY: Yes, ten thousand scudi...

GIUSEPPINA: He's finally gone mad.

DOROTEA: [*To TOGNINO*] Go and find the master.

TOGNINO: *Sissignora.*

DOROTEA: [*To TOGNINO*] Shift yourself!

TOGNINO: [*On his way out*] (How to warn Valentina?)

NOTARY: As I was coming upstairs, if I was not mistaken, I thought I saw the padrone coming into the courtyard.

DOROTEA: Come with me: I want to speak to him. If he comes back like a madman, talking of convents, rat me, but I can hand out punishment to suit. [*She goes out*]

GIUSEPPINA: Come, Signor Fulgenzio, I want to hear what my uncle has to say. If he wants to give that worthless woman a dowry, he will have to get it from me; but only if the judge tears up that bit of paper. My aunt makes a deal of noise, but I prefer deeds to words. [*She goes*]

FULGENZIO: Come, signor Notary.

NOTARY: Where to?

FULGENZIO: Come with us; your efforts will be recompensed. (The twinkling of an eye can bring order out of disorder) [*He goes*]

NOTARY: (There would seem a fine imbroglio afoot. Enough that I get paid; I don't look for anything else) [*He goes*]

IPPOLITO: They've left us alone.

ROSINA: Then let us go as well.

IPPOLITO: Couldn't I stay with you for just a little?

ROSINA: Signor, it would not be suitable; not before we're married.

IPPOLITO: Sweetheart, I see scant chance of that.

[*They leave. A pause; there is thunder in the air; then VALENTINA enters*]

VALENTINA: What do I hear? Small comfort that Tognino told me
everything. They know about my marriage, and so far believe the master
approves of it; but if they blurt it out to him, how can I explain the
contract? I have it, I could hide it... but he would see a mystery. An ugly
impasse. Oh, sister, sister, why were you born? You brought on this
disaster. As long as I was on my own, I stayed in this place, bettering my
fortune step by step. Then she, from love, or more probably interest,
edges me off the straight road. For the evil we do, Heaven makes us mad
and blind. Climbing out of one abyss, we find ourselves falling into
another. What will become of me, of her, of Baldissera now? If I lose the
master's good graces, I lose my reputation in the eyes of the world. Have
I worked this hard in this house to gain respect, to be forced to leave it
dishonoured? They're coming. If I survive this, I shall live a penitent
the rest of my days. They say: once past the lighthouse, the sailor forgets
the danger. But not me; if I can just save my reputation... [*She goes out.
The others return*]

FULGENZIO: He wants us to wait here.

DOROTEA: I ain't leaving anyway, if I have to wait till morning.

GIUSEPPINA: Where is Valentina? I don't see her anywhere.

DOROTEA: Doubtless with her darling husband, consummating the
great day.

IPPOLITO: Just what I plan to do.

ROSINA: Here is my uncle: speak to him.

IPPOLITO: Oh, I'd be too shy.

FABRIZIO: [*Entering*] Such distinguished company!

DOROTEA: And tired of waiting.

FABRIZIO: Then take yourself off: I've nothing to say to you.

GIUSEPPINA: Come on now, we are not here to grumble.

FABRIZIO: Tomorrow you will be on your way to the nunnery.

DOROTEA: (My fingers are itching)

GIUSEPPINA: So I am destined for the nunnery. And Rosina, Signore?

FABRIZIO: Rosina is married.

GIUSEPPINA: Before me?

FABRIZIO: What's done is done. And here is the very lawyer who drew up the contract.

NOTARY: I, signor? That is not so.

FABRIZIO: What? Are you drunk?

NOTARY: Signor! I am a man of reputation. The contract I drew up was not for these two, as you very well know.

FABRIZIO: Damnation! For whom, then?

NOTARY: If you now wish to marry the signora Rosina I can draw up the relevant documents.

FABRIZIO: [To the NOTARY] Hold your tongue. [Looking about him] Where is Valentina? Valentina, where are you? (I feel my heart pounding) Valentina! Call her.

VALENTINA: [Entering] I am here, signore.

FABRIZIO: [Indicating the NOTARY] What's this fellow saying?

VALENTINA: Hear me out in peace, signor; I will explain. I was born in dire poverty; dealt a bad hand by Fate, to better myself I went into service, and in this house, at the cost of gruelling hard work, I arrived where I am. What did I not do, signore, to acquire respect? To be accepted? I was ready to serve everyone; not even the mistresses could complain of my work. But Fate cruelly decreed I should be loved by you, and returning your love made me hated. Hate bred hate; I repaid vengeance with vengeance, sowing discord through the house. But that is the least fault: my shame, yet more aroused, was fanned into flame by a reckless love; Baldissera's eyes had won me. Hiding from you the fire in my heart, I made myself over-pleasing in your eyes. A poor girl, with no means of support, ill-advised, tried to make her fortune: but my heart was swayed by comfort, fear of poverty and that over-daring love that believed Felicita when she said I should marry him. I married Baldissera under your very eyes. The contract was for me. I read it out to you, changing the names: I am ten thousand scudi richer at your expense; I am ready to give it back. I came here poor, I shall go away poor; I hate my deceit and my idiotic pride. I deserve punishment. At your feet, an ungrateful woman asks forgiveness. [Kneels at FABRIZIO's feet]

FABRIZIO: [Displaying confusion, the conflict between rage and love clearly visible] Wicked creature!... (I am so wretched!) Leave my house... (This is torture!) Damn you!... Get up... (How beautiful you are!)

DOROTEA: Very fine, your ladyship!

GIUSEPPINA: Valentina, such strength of character!

VALENTINA: Enough, signora, I am sufficiently humiliated. Charity teaches us not to scorn the oppressed. We all need to look into our hearts.

FELICITA: [*Entering with BALDISSERA*] Sister, what is going on?

BALDISSERA: What's happening, sister-in-law?

FABRIZIO: [*To FELICITA and BALDISSERA*] Get out of here, you rogue. And you, you insolent baggage.

BALDISSERA: This to me? What have I done?

FELICITA: To me? Are you mad?

VALENTINA: Sister, they know Baldissera is my husband. Since it was your ill-advice persuaded me to that step, you can share my ill-fortune.

BALDISSERA: [*To VALENTINA*] The dowry?

VALENTINA: Whatever I have in the world, I wish to give back to the master.

BALDISSERA: [*To FELICITA*] Then you can give me back that bond.

VALENTINA: What bond?

BALDISSERA: She robbed me of four hundred scudi - to get you to marry me. And the notary witnessed it.

NOTARY: I only did what I was asked.

VALENTINA: [*To FELICITA*] Give him the bond.

FELICITA: [*Giving it to BALDISSERA and leaving*] Use it to wipe your... nose.

DOROTEA: [*To FABRIZIO*] Well now, signore, what are we to do about all this?

FABRIZIO: Don't, you'll split my head.

DOROTEA: We'll provide for ourselves, then. We'll see in a few hours who can do more in Milan, you or the Governor.

FABRIZIO: Don't pester me any more, do what you like. Go, just go to the devil, all the lot of you. [*To VALENTINA*] Oh, you witch!

VALENTINA: (But he still loves me)

DOROTEA: Come, nieces, we must decide. Here is the lawyer ready; we are not short of witnesses. Without pestering your precious uncle, let us finally have a little marrying.

[*The NOTARY takes down the names of the two couples*]

FABRIZIO: [*In tears, to VALENTINA*] How could you have the heart?... You traitor!

BALDISSERA: [*Aside to VALENTINA*] (He's coming round)

VALENTINA: (I'm not working that way again)

BALDISSERA: (We have to eat)

VALENTINA: (Work)

BALDISSERA: (*Basta.* One can but try)
VALENTINA: (If you're a gentleman, Heaven will provide)
BALDISSERA: (At least try and get something to live on for a bit)
VALENTINA: (The ring? The hundred scudi?)
BALDISSERA: (Gone)
VALENTINA: (Gambling? Oh, damn you, Felicita! To cheat me even in that!)
DOROTEA: Well, signor Notary, spread out the contracts. The bargains and conditions are already understood. Now, not to make a complete waste of the day, all four young people are ready to give their hands.
GIUSEPPINA: Uncle, are you content?
FABRIZIO: [*Angry*] Yes, yes, I give my permission.
FULGENZIO: Your permission, uncle?
FABRIZIO: Yes!
ROSINA: Signore, will you give me away?
FABRIZIO: Yes, yes, I said I would.
IPPOLITO: Will you do me the honour?...
FABRIZIO: They're doing it for spite.
[*He stamps his foot, to IPPOLITO's alarm*]
DOROTEA: No need for threats! Do you not yet know the man's a beast?
IPPOLITO: A beast? A beast?
DOROTEA: Be kind, be human. Come, let us finish this; give your hands.
FULGENZIO: [*Giving his hand to GIUSEPPINA*] You are mine.
GIUSEPPINA: Yours.
IPPOLITO: [*To ROSINA*] My hand.
ROSINA: Take it.
DOROTEA: [*Indicating FABRIZIO*] Now get a hundred miles away from that demon.
[*All leave except FABRIZIO, BALDISSERA and VALENTINA*]
FABRIZIO: I am no demon, I am a dead man, murdered by that ungrateful wretch. Savage, have you no heart? No compassion?
[*BALDISSERA makes angry signs to VALENTINA to be reconciled*]
VALENTINA: Now I am married, signore, honour demands I too should leave this house, along with my husband. I wish to follow the custom of honourable wives. I shall always remember the benefits you showed me. What I acquired wickedly, I will restore penitently.
FABRIZIO: No, take it all. I want nothing from you. Enjoy it all in peace. May Heaven grant you that happiness which, because of you, I can no

longer hope for. I forgive you everything, I wipe out the offenses, the debts - but - come to see me though, shall we say twice a month?

VALENTINA: I willingly accept your generous invitation. Yes, I shall come to see you, and shall I bring my husband?

[*She steps forward to address the audience*]

I must ask pardon from all concerned, and forgiveness from all of you. If there have been housekeepers among those listening, they will have censured me, and not without reason. But between the theatre and the home there is a great gulf fixed. Our situations, dreamt up by our author and placed under the glare of lights, how could they bear any relation to any real persons or actual happenings? All of us know how chock-full the world is of really good women. Let us be thankful for that.

## THE END